# THE PRINCE
# OF DARKNESS

*Frontispiece: French Engraving, c 1670.*
Warburg Institute

# THE PRINCE OF DARKNESS

### THE DEVIL IN HISTORY, RELIGION
### AND THE HUMAN PSYCHE

## JOAN O'GRADY

BARNES
&NOBLE
BOOKS
NEW YORK

*To Selina*
*Critic and Encourager*

# Contents

# THE PRINCE
# OF DARKNESS

# Introduction

The image of a Prince of Darkness, terrifying opponent of gods and men, has existed in the human mind, through countless ages and among numerous nations and races. This image has appeared under many guises and, under many guises, still continues to exist. Such a time-honoured and universally held conception might point to the possibility of a demonic presence actually operating in our world. On the other hand, it might merely suggest the existence of some fundamental tendency in the human psyche – the tendency to create an imaginary enemy to explain seemingly insoluble problems. Whichever way it is taken, an idea of such universality cannot be ignored.

This 'dark enemy' enters into many different religions, and the folklores of all continents. It is important, therefore, to know from where we, of the West, inherit our understanding and picture of 'him'. Most of us, when we use the term 'Devil' to describe this enemy, are not at all certain what we mean by the term or what we believe about it. This applies to those with religious beliefs, as well as to those without them. The first thing to do, then, is to explore the historical origins, developments and changes in ideas about this being, both in religious teachings, in the general outlook of succeeding periods, and in the historical consequences of belief or disbelief in 'him'.

The 'Prince of Darkness' can also be studied in philosophy, in art and literature, in medicine and psychiatry, and in occultism of every kind. Above all, 'he' can be studied in one's own personal experience. Whether 'he' is treated as symbol or as fact, as a concept or as an existence, there are innumerable aspects of 'him' to be encountered. Discussion of these may possibly help in approaching this question of symbol or fact. It will, at any rate, show how many tangled complications surround the concept of 'the Prince of Darkness', and make that title a most apt description of 'him'.

# CHAPTER 1

# The Devil in Ancient Myth and Jewish Tradition

A battle between Light and Darkness, between Creation and Destruction was the ancient picture of the universe as conceived by the human mind from the beginning of recorded times. The obscurity of Darkness and the clarity of Light were seen as two fundamental antagonists. The idea of this cosmic conflict gave rise to the religious myths of many ancient civilisations; and, connected with this idea, involved with it but not necessarily the same, was the conception of the battle within humanity itself, between the forces of good and the forces of evil.

Theologians and philosophers have long struggled to define and analyse the *meaning* of evil. But before any definitions had been evolved, this conception of a struggle between creation and destruction, between growth and opposition to growth had affected most religious interpretations of the world and coloured many philosophical theories.

The idea of universal conflict has been expressed in numerous different ways and has entered the stories and legends of peoples of all times and places. Myths describing the conflict belong not only to ancient and profound religious systems but also to primitive communities of all eras. Their experiences of the harsh forces of nature, forces they saw to be infinitely more powerful than themselves, caused them to people their world with evil spirits, who were trying to do them harm. The figures of demons have had a long existence in the human mind. For protection, men would turn to good spirits or, more often, to the greatest of the good spirits, who, they felt, would surely fight for them. The chief adversary of this good spirit would then be conceived by them as the author of all the ills that beset their world.

It has been found that many of the myths belonging not only to great religions, but also to primitive peoples and to primitive societies of the present day, include a story of a wicked being coming into the world to destroy the work of the good being who had created it. It seems that human beings have in all ages and in all places been struggling to explain how so much that is evil has managed to insert itself into a world made and ruled by a supreme being who should be the object of worship.

From the earliest times known to history, up to and including the present, the problem of how evil could have entered a world created good has been pondered and discussed, dealt with in myth and metaphor, in theology and philosophy, and seems to be one of the greatest sources of religious doubt in people's minds today. How can the misery and wickedness to which all can testify exist in a world made by an all-loving God? Exactly what the focal point of evil is, and what its power, and how its existence can be explained, no one knows for sure, but what is certain is that the idea of an enemy of gods and men is a very ancient and all-pervasive one.

The concept of the Enemy as known to Western Europe has come to us mainly through the Scriptures of the Jewish people, whose terminology and imagery were influenced by the older civilisations that surrounded them. We have inherited this concept, so it is important for us to have an idea of how it was formed and how it developed.

In one of the civilisations with which the Jewish people came into contact – the Babylonian – there was a myth concerning the origin of our world. This myth is known as the Epic of Creation. It tells of the creation of the world out of the primeval deep and of the birth of the gods of light. The centre of the story is the struggle between the gods of light and the powers of darkness. Bel-Meridach, the hero-god, responsible for the earth, was in mortal combat with Tiamat, the Dragon of Chaos. The Dragon, the force trying to destroy the order of the universe, was the opposer of the Creator-God. If undefeated, he would reduce all world-order to chaos and nothingness. But Bel-Meridach conquers.

The myths and symbols of Babylonia greatly influenced the writings of the Jewish people. Words and images connected with Babylonian symbols can be found in the Old Testament. The most obvious of these is the Leviathan, the Dragon. 'In that day the Lord with his sore and great and strong sword shall punish Leviathan, the piercing serpent, even Leviathan, the crooked serpent; and he shall slay the Dragon that is in the sea' (Isaiah 27:1). Out of these symbols grew much of the imagery formed round the later concept of the Evil One, the inducer of disorder and chaos.

Another ancient religious culture which was later to have a powerful and lasting influence on Jewish writers was that of Persia. It was from here that there came a theology entirely based on the opposing forces of good and evil. The dualism of this religion was to have an influence that lasted through the centuries.

Zoroaster was known in antiquity as the founder of the Magian System, the religion of the Magi, which became the accepted religion of the Persio-Iranian people. In this system, the principle of evil was wholly separate from the principle of the Divine. It was held that everything has a cause, and, since good cannot cause evil, therefore evil is a separate principle.

The natural world emanated from the wise Lord, Ahura Mazda or Ormazd, the primordial Spirit Being. His guiding spirit continually willed the good but was restricted by his own twin brother, the evil spirit, Ahriman. Ahriman was banished by the good spirit and now lives in Hell, from where he invades the world as the principle of evil, the arch-devil. The evil spirit existed in the cosmos from the beginning and has negative creative powers, bringing darkness, filth and death. The good spirit is the essence of truth and law. The history of the world is the history of the conflict between Ormazd and Ahriman, but it is their creatures, men and demons respectively, who must do the actual fighting. The world is the battlefield. Man is at the centre, and his soul is the object of the war. He has been given free will, which makes him accessible to the evil spirit, though he can call on Ormazd for help. The absolute independent principle of evil became personified in Ahriman, but the original conception in the Zoroastrian religion was probably not a complete dualism. Zoroaster had taught that the primordial Spirit Being was above the two opposing spirits, and that their conflict existed only in the epoch of time which belongs to our world, and is of small duration when taken in the scale of universal history. At the end of this world, Ahriman will be overcome and cast into the abyss of Hell for ever.

The essence of Ahriman was falsehood, and that of Ormazd was truth. It was this conception of eternal conflict as the central meaning of religion itself that had such great effect on religious teachings and doctrines of later times. And Ahriman, the deceiver, who was cast out of Heaven and thrust into Hell, is clearly akin to the Jewish conception of the Enemy, the Arch-deceiver.

The fact that religious myths of other civilisations influenced the Jews in the terminology they used, and, therefore, often in their concepts of the Enemy, does not mean that their theology of evil was a borrowed one. The development and growth of their religion was integral to the early history of the Jewish people, and this development was their great contribution to world civilisation. Because our ideas of the Devil have very largely come through them, it is important to find out more about early Jewish thought and tradition. The conception of the Devil, which we of the West have inherited from their thoughts and beliefs, has played its powerful part in our language and literature, in the history of nations and in the lives of individuals, however much we, today, may do our best to water it down.

Although the principle that there is an evil force in the universe, fighting against the good, appears in the myths of so many ancient civilisations, the earliest known religious writings of these civilisations often show a rather different conception of good and evil. In these accounts, everything comes from the hand of the Supreme Lord and Creator, and therefore, both what to us seems to be good and what seems to be evil are sent by him. The gods of ancient Egypt had this ambivalence. They all shared the majesty of a supreme god, who handed out both good and evil, being the author of all things. In their early myths, the god, Set, was identified with destruction, the death of the sun through the murder of Osiris; but he was also venerated as a great and powerful god-creator. In the myths of later Egypt, the story of Set was simplified, so that he became a purely wicked being, hostile to all men; in fact, he developed into the personification of evil. And this conception may also have contributed to later biblical ideas of the Enemy, through the influence of Egypt on the Jewish people.

The absence of a single principle of evil is seen more especially in Hinduism, which is and has remained a very metaphysical religion. It is again a very ancient one, probably the most ancient of all known religions. Despite its huge pantheon of gods, Hinduism regards its deities as manifestations of the One, and ascribes to them powers of destruction as well as of creation, of death as well as of life. The greater part of Hindu mythology, as in many other mythologies, is concerned with a cosmic battle and the spiritual combat between Light and Darkness. But despite this central idea of universal conflict, there is no portrayal of a figure that is the focus of evil. Kali, the goddess of death who devours everything, is the obverse side of the mother goddess, who nourishes all living beings. The ferocious aspect of Kali has led, in popular worship, to her portrayal as the cruel black goddess of destruction and terror. But in Hindu mythology she is very far from being a concept of the Devil. There is no tendency to dualism.

The concept of the One Supreme God, was also the centre of the Jewish faith, and distinguished the early Hebrew religion from the religions of the neighbouring peoples, with their numerous tribal gods.

In the earliest Jewish scriptures, Yahweh was Lord of the Universe, and all happenings, good and evil, were caused by him. In Isaish 45:7, written in the sixth century BC, God says, 'I form the Light and create darkness. I make peace and create evil. I, the Lord, do all these things.'

Later, it began to be felt that God, the author of all good, should not be described as the cause of evil; there must be a separate cause. The Persian religion, with which the Jews came into contact during the Babylonian exile, was clearly the influence behind this type of thinking. Evil was increasingly understood to come from an enemy, who opposed God and Man – the Adversary, which is the meaning of the Hebrew word 'Satan'.

In the Book of Job, Satan appears as the accuser and tempter of Man, but he is still seen as a subject of the World Ruler. He comes before the heavenly court as one of the sons of God and acts under the Lord's instructions.

In the Book of Samuel, compiled in the tenth century BC, it

is written: 'The Lord tempted Samuel.' But in a much later Old Testament book, 1 Chronicles (21:1) it is Satan who tempts David to disobey the Law and incur the wrath of God. The danger was now understood not to come through God but from the Enemy. By the second century BC, the two sides of God were no longer emphasised in Jewish religious stories and histories. It may be that in this period the ethics of religion seemed more important than the metaphysics: God should no longer be connected with anything other than good.

Yet, many centuries later, the ancient Jewish conception of Yahweh was again expressed. In the Cabbala (a medieval Jewish theosophical system), it was said that Yahweh, who was all, contained everything – good and evil. His right hand gave mercy, his left, destruction. But the destructive aspect broke away and became known as the Devil.

A better-known mythological explanation of how the evil principle entered our world had its first appearance in the Book of Enoch, an Apocryphal book, written about 200 BC. This was the story of the Fall of Angels – the entrance into our world of the Prince of Darkness.

The story of how Satan was cast out of heaven comes, as far as we know, from the Jewish Apocryphal books. These were writings circulating among the Jews during the centuries just before and just after the beginning of the Christian era. The most important of these was the Book of Enoch.

The Book of Enoch was, in fact, a collection of literary works, appearing under the name of Enoch, but written by many different writers. It was apparently well known until the eighth century, and then it seems to have completely disappeared. Centuries later, at the end of the eighteenth century, one version was found in Abyssinia. It was written in the Ethiopian language and seems to have been a translation from a Greek original which has never been discovered. Another version, known as 'The Secrets of Enoch', was found in Russia in a Slavonic text, and translated into English in the nineteenth century.

The story of the Fall of Angels is not properly a scriptural doctrine, in that it never entered into the orthodox body of Old Testament writings. And yet it was to form the main basis of later teachings about Satan and his place in our world.

In the Apocryphal story, the history of the angels was revealed to Enoch. He was shown how, from the heavenly court, a group of angels, encouraged by their leader, descended to earth. There they 'lusted after the daughters of men' and rejected heaven, becoming evil fallen beings, the Watcher Angels, who produced a race of giants from the 'daughters of men'. This part of the story seems to be connected with Genesis 6.

The Watchers taught men arts and sciences, but also vice. Their offspring 'spread iniquity on earth' till God caused the Flood, as punishment for sinful human beings, and chained the angels to the dark places of earth until the Last Judgement. But the giants had produced offspring, evil spirits, who remained, and continued to lead men astray. Four protector angels of whom Michael was one, were sent to fight for men.

The other book, the Book of the Secrets of Enoch, written probably in Egypt at the beginning of the Christian era, tells of Enoch's journey through the different courts of Heaven. He is shown the Grigori in prison. They were rebel angels who, with their prince, Satanael, had rejected the Holy Lord. And the Lord says, 'One of these in the ranks of Archangels . . . entertained the impossible idea . . . that he should be equal in rank io my power. And I hurled him from the heights.'

The Apocalyptic books, written between the first century BC and the first century AD, were primarily prophetic revelations of the future of Israel and the world. In these books, teachings about the Evil Angel grew ever more specific.

In the Book of the Twelve Patriarchs, one of the Apocryphal books, Belial is the name of the chief of the Fallen Angels. He is the antagonist of God and competes for the allegiance of men. He says, 'Do you choose light or darkness, the Law of the Lord or the works of Belial?' In the Apocalyptic Book of Jubilees, it is told that the Watchers came to earth and then sinned, but that their prince, Sammael, was allowed by Jehovah to harass humankind.

Gradually, the numerous names used to describe leaders of the rebel angels coalesced into the name of one spiritual being, personifying the origin and essence of all evil. Satan, the adversary, became the most important and the most often used of all names for this being.

In the story of the Fall of Angels, the great archangel who rebelled had been a good and mighty being. Through his own rejection of good, he brought evil into the universe.

How this evil was to enter the world of men has been

portrayed in another story – that of Adam and Eve and the Fall of Man. This story is certainly part of the Jewish Scriptures. The first and second books of the Old Testament, Genesis 1 and 11 (by Jewish tradition ascribed to Moses), describe Man in his primeval position in the Garden of Eden, living as he was meant to live. Sin intervened in the form of the Serpent, who told Eve that, through eating from the Tree of the Knowledge of Good and Evil, she and Adam, as human beings, could be equal with the Elohim who had made them. Then they would see that living for their own personal satisfaction was the ultimate purpose of their creation.

For the early Jewish writers, the Serpent was a symbolic representation of tempting power. It was later that he was made equivalent to Satan. But the story again shows beings created good, and, through their own fault, falling from their primal state. From that moment on, it is written in Genesis, there would be permanent conflict between humankind and the Serpent; sin and death had come into our world.

In order to express ideas about cosmic happenings on a huge scale, of which it is impossible to have direct knowledge, all great religions, without exception, have had recourse to myth. It is the only way. So the fact that similar myths, describing a universal struggle between good and evil, appear in many religions, and the fact that, in Hebrew Scriptures, there are stories especially devised to give an explanation of the coming of evil does not mean that the Devil himself is necessarily a work of human fantasy. That a conception of him has appeared in all periods and in innumerable places neither proves nor disproves anything about him.

It is not only simple people who confuse the meanings that a myth is used to convey with the actual events in the story; even the most learned tend to do this. The debates and discussions about evil and the focal point of evil that have continued throughout history show how often this takes place. There has always been a tendency to confuse belief in the principle embodied in a religious myth with belief in the actual events that are said to have happened. They are obviously not the same. This confusion has led to many sterile arguments and to many attacks on religious belief in general, equating it with superstition. The danger of this confusion constantly appears in questions concerning the Devil. All that has been written about him in religious systems and in countless legends and stories makes it difficult to separate metaphor from what is meant to be description of fact.

The story of Adam and Eve describes how the evils of sin and death came into the world, and it also shows how the Enemy can attack each individual. If Man has free will, he is able to listen and possibly to succumb to a tempter. The idea of a battle between good and evil on the stage of the world had appeared in many religions, but the portrayal of an attack on individual human beings gave to Jewish scriptures another dimension in the story of the Devil.

In Buddhism, which had its beginnings in the sixth century BC, the Evil One is shown primarily as the Tempter. In some of the writings telling of the life of the Buddha, Mara, the great Tempter, is said to have appeared to him in the sky and to have tried to stop him from renouncing his worldly life and setting out to become a wanderer. The words of Mara had no effect, but the story adds that as a shadow always follows the body, so he too, from that day, always followed the Blessed One, striving to throw every obstacle in his way towards the Buddhahood. At the crucial moment of the Buddha's life, when seated in meditation beneath the Sacred Bo Tree, Mara appears again to tempt him and persuade him to give up his mission. The Buddha has to struggle and overcome.

Mara is also called Varsavati, 'he who fulfils desires'. For the desire or thirst for pleasure, for power, even for existence links human beings to the ever-turning wheel of life and prevents escape to true being, or Nirvana. In the Dhammapada, a fourth or fifth century collection of Buddhist ethical verses, Mara is the personification of evil: 'He who is looking for pleasure only, his senses uncontrolled . . . Mara will certainly overthrow, as the wind throws down a feeble tree.'

Buddhist teachings spread as far as Persia and so the conception of Mara, the Tempter, though by no means central to Buddhism, entered the Zoroastrian religion and thus reached the Jews in Babylon – yet another influence on their thinking. The Jewish writings of the post-exilic period show the Tempter and the Adversary as one. Earlier, Satan, in his role of Tempter, was described, in a certain sense, as working under the power of God. Now, in post-exilic times, the meaning of Satan as 'adversary' included all his attributed functions, and these were said to oppose the aims of God and Man.

In the Apocalyptic books of the centuries just before the

Christian era, appellations of the Enemy were beginning to coalesce. The serpent of Genesis was for the first time in literature identified with Satan, the Devil. Our word, 'Devil' is derived from the Greek 'Diabolos', accuser or assailant. When, between the years 285 and 247 BC, the Old Testament was translated into the Greek version, known as the Septuagint, 'Diabolos' was the word translated from the Hebrew word, 'Satan', meaning 'adversary'.

Beelzebub and Belial were other names used for Satan in the Apocalyptic period of Hebrew scripture. The name Beelzebub is mentioned only once in the Old Testament. In 2 Kings 1, the King of Israel sends messengers to enquire of Beelzebub, the god of Ekron, whether he would recover from his sickness. The angel of the Lord tells Elijah to rebuke the king, saying: 'Is there no God in Israel to enquire of his word? Therefore thou . . . shalt surely die.'

'Baal', 'lord' was the title given to a local deity; 'zebub' means 'flies'. Beelzebub, therefore, could be: the Baal to whom flies are holy – the Lord of the Flies. Divination by means of flies was known to be practised in Babylon.

In some versions of the New Testament, the name 'Beelzebul' is used. The word 'zebul' appears in Kings, expressing height; 'beth-zebul' is the high house, or temple, so Beelzebul could be 'Lord of the High House'. Matthew 10:25 has: 'If they have called the Master of the house Beelzebul, how much more shall they call them of his household?'

But whether he is written as Beelzebub or Beelzebul nothing is known as to how or when this particular pagan god became the 'prince of devils' (Mark 3:22), though it was very usual for the Jews of Old Testament times to regard the heathen gods of their neighbours as representations of the Evil One.

The name, 'Belial', though absent from the literature of the orthodox Jewish Rabbis, figured often in Apocryphal literature as the Prince of Evil. By the beginning of the Christian era, all these names belonged to one figure – Satan, the Prince of Darkness – and he was the Tempter, the Accuser, the Adversary.

Despite his long ancestry and his continual appearance in the Apocryphal and Apocalyptic books, the Old Testament itself has relatively little in it specifically about the Devil. Nevertheless, the Jewish people were clearly familiar with the idea of his existence, as can be seen in the New Testament. In the New Testament, the Devil figures prominently, and it is from the sayings in the New Testament that the idea of the Devil and his minions was developed. This idea entered into the Christianity of succeeding ages, and so into the life and legend of the West.

# CHAPTER 2

# The Devil of the New Testament and the Church Fathers

The Jewish people, who listened to the first Christian teaching, were clearly accustomed to think that there existed an Evil Spirit who opposed God and Man, and was Lord over innumerable lesser devils. This was language that they understood. The Jews of that period felt themselves to be living in a world peopled with angels and demons.

The Christian religion has developed the idea of the Devil more extensively than any other world religion. It is remarkable how many times the word translated as 'devil' is used in the Gospels, far more often than in other religious scriptures. It may not always have exactly the same meaning, and it may appear in different contexts and have different degrees of importance, but it is certainly very often there. And the cure and restoration of suffering people by the casting out of devils plays a very great part in the Gospel story.

This emphasis on the power of the forces of Darkness may have been given such an important place because Christianity was less a religion of metaphysics than a religion of action: 'What is the most important thing in Christ's teaching? It is *action*: do this, do not do that . . . You must take Christianity as a teaching of action, not as a mental teaching'. (P. D. Ouspensky, *The Fourth Way*). The followers of Christianity were taught what they should do and what they should resist in order to achieve their goal. Their friends and their enemies were shown to them.

In the Epistles and in the Apocalypse of Saint John, the idea of the Devil as the Arch-enemy is made even more definite. The most powerful description of the Enemy of *Man* comes in the Epistle of Peter (1 Peter 5:8): 'Be sober, be diligent; because your adversary, the Devil, as a roaring lion, walketh about, seeking whom he may devour.' Yet it is perhaps only Saint Paul who has written a statement about the focus of evil that it is impossible to interpret in a symbolic way as a metaphor for human sinfulness. 'Put on the whole armour of God, that ye may be able to stand against the wiles of the Devil. *For we wrestle not against flesh and blood*, but against principalities, against powers, against the rulers of the darkness of this world, against spiritual wickedness in high places' (Ephesians 6:12; my italics).

In The Apocalypse (The Revelation of St John), the Devil is shown as the Enemy of *God*. Revelation makes use of the language of the Book of Enoch and of the post-exilic Old Testament – language also reminiscent of the ancient Babylonian mythology. 'And the great dragon was cast out, that old serpent, called the Devil and Satan, which deceiveth the whole world, he was cast out into the earth and his angels were cast out with him.' (Revelation 12:9). It is on Revelation 12 that the later Christian theology of Satan's fall from Heaven and his continual opposition to the Divine Plan is based.

The Church Fathers studied the words of the Book of Revelation and made the Devil completely synonymous with the Fallen Angel who had disobeyed God. But this equation was never directly made in the Gospels, and, as has been seen, the story of the Fallen Angels was not a scriptural doctrine of the Old Testament. Already, in the first century, Ignatius, the martyred bishop of Antioch, spoke of 'the Satan' as the leader of the evil Angels, though it was through Origen, an Alexandrian writer and teacher at the end of the second century, that the traditional view of the Devil has mainly come.

The name of 'Lucifer' does not appear in the New Testament. In speaking of the power given to the disciples over the power of the enemy, Christ said, 'I beheld Satan, as lightning fall from Heaven' (Luke 10:18). In Revelation 9, a star fell from Heaven and became Appollyon, the angel of the bottomless pit. These sayings were held by Origen and later Church Fathers to refer to the chapter in Isaiah where Yahweh is protecting his people by overthrowing the pride of their enemy: 'How art thou fallen from Heaven, O Lucifer, son of the morning! how art thou cut down to the ground, . . . for thou hast said in thine heart, "I will ascend into heaven, I will exalt my throne above the stars of God" ' (Isaiah 14:12–13). 'Lucifer' was then taken to be the name of Satan before his Fall from Heaven. The higher the being, the greater the fall. Lucifer, the light-bearer, had become the Prince of Darkness.

According to Origen, Lucifer and his angels fell through their own free choice. Their motive was pride, aiming to equate themselves with God. They desired to put their own will in the place of God's will; this was understood to be the basis of sin on every level. Gradually, these ideas began to form the traditional teachings on the Devil.

The Church Fathers regarded the struggle between fulfilment of a Divine Plan and the opposition to it as central to the history of the universe. They aimed, as did the teachers of all great religions, to describe and explain a cosmic conflict. By the end of the fourth century, this conflict was portrayed by the Church as the battle of Christ against the Devil and his minions.

In orthodox Christianity, the Devil's power was always shown to be limited by God. Christian theology held the Devil to have been created by God as a great and good being, but, by his own volition, turning to evil. Orthodox Christianity never made evil an equal and independent principle. But though the Devil was described as subordinate to God, and, in a sense, fulfilling His purpose, still the Apostolic Fathers wrote of the Enemy as locked in a cosmic struggle with the Saviour of Mankind. Satan, though created good by God, through his fall, had become the leader of the evil forces in the Cosmos.

In the very early days of Christianity, there was a belief among some Christians that God had established two kingdoms, one belonging to Christ, and the other to the Devil. To the former belonged the heavenly Kingdom of the world to come, to the latter the present world. St Ignatius called the Devil 'the ruler of this age', and in some of the first Christian writings, such as the 'Letters of Barnabas' and the 'Shepherd of Hermas', the struggle between the two kingdoms is made central to the Christian outlook on life.

The Gospel words, 'The Prince of this world' (John, 12:31 and 14:30), used to describe the opponent of Christ, had, for the Church Fathers, very great importance. It underlined the conception of the Devil as master of the present world. The term, 'the world' was chiefly used by the Church Fathers to mean 'attachment to the world'. Satan's mastery was, therefore, not over the world as such, but over the worldlings who, through their attachments, had made themselves part of the Devil's army. The greatest exponent of this meaning of the two kingdoms was St Augustine.

In one of his most famous books, *The City of God*, he describes the Cosmos as divided into an earthly and a heavenly city. Evil angels and evil human beings occupy the evil city and good angels and good human beings the heavenly one. But the world we live in is a mixture of the two, and we cannot tell who belongs to which kingdom; we cannot even be sure for ourselves, as we constantly change. Satan holds in his power those who prefer the evil city.

The problem of evil held a central place in St Augustine's writings. He believed that God allowed evil powers to rule the world, but within His control, as part of the 'plot' of the Cosmos. Especially after the horror of the Fall of Rome, in AD 410, St Augustine saw the world as being under the vast power of the Devil, but always he conceived evil to be the result of a definite choice, no creature having been created evil. Satan had chosen evil and for ever works to destroy the Cosmos.

The Gospels of the New Testament did *not* give a metaphysical account of evil and of how evil entered the world; they showed how evil can affect each human being, and how each human being can fight against it – in fact, how to fight temptation.

The most important scene in which the Devil is shown in his role as Tempter is given in the account of the Temptation in the Wilderness. Satan tries, by holding out false values, to deceive and destroy, and he is overcome. The meaning of the story may be clear, but it is not clear how literally the figure of the Devil is meant to be understood.

The Devil is said to have entered into Judas (John 13:2 and 27), and Christ says that Peter was in danger of falling into Satan's hands (Luke 22:31). But again it is difficult to know in what sense these sayings are used. So the Gospel teaching itself does not give any certainty as to whether the Devil is an independent spirit existing in the universe, or whether he should be regarded as the symbolic expression of those things that are sinful or lead to sin. It was the development of Christian doctrine by the Church Fathers out of the teachings of Scripture that defined the concept of the Devil as a definite ontological being.

In the many stories of healing, the casting out of devils is described as the cure, sometimes of an infirmity, sometimes of possession or madness, sometimes of evil forces within, and, in all cases, as having a deeper and more universal meaning than a particular cure of a particular disease. The twelve disciples were given power to cast out devils, and it is clear from their failure to cure the epileptic boy (Luke 9:37–42) that the existence of different kinds of devil, needing different kinds of treatment was clearly understood. But this does not help in the understanding of what Satan actually is.

The most important of all Gospel sayings about the Devil comes in John 8:44: 'He was a murderer from the beginning and abode not in the truth, because there is no truth in him. When he speaketh a lie, he speaketh of his own; for he is a liar and the father of it.' Perhaps this saying, more than any other saying or story, can give help in understanding how the Devil is treated in the Gospels. The Deception, the Illusion, the Lie, in all religions, constitute the Enemy.

In religious teaching, this Lie, which is the Enemy, consists in the portrayal of the world and man's position in it upside-down: what is good is seen to be bad, what is bad is seen to be good; what is important, unimportant, and what is unimportant, important. Each person is made to hold the arbitrary assumption that he has an automatic *right* to happiness; and a human being is made to assume that he consists only of his ego and that ego to be of godlike consequence. How these lies entered the human consciousness and there set up the greatest obstacle to human development it was hard for religious teachers to explain, unless they showed them to have come from the Devil, the Father of Lies.

The presentation of evil under the guise of good is at the heart of 'the Devil's work'. The story of Adam and Eve centres on this deception. The Serpent deceived the woman by making her think that the natural human mind could attain godlike omniscience, and that this false assumption of universal knowledge is its greatest good. In some versions of the story – in the Apocryphal Old Testament – the Serpent appeared to Eve as an angel of light. The deception was accepted, bringing a mortal flaw into the human psyche – it became for ever open to suggestion leading downwards, and to an ingrained view of the world that was opposed to reality.

The Gnostic Apocryphal Book, 'The Acts of Peter', describes the result of this lie in a speech made by St Peter to his executioners:

> I beseech you, the executioners, crucify me thus, with the head downward and not otherwise: and the reason wherefore I will tell unto them that hear. . . .
>
> Learn ye the mystery of all nature, and the beginning of all things, what it was. For the first man, of the race of whom I bear the likeness, fell head downwards and showed forth a manner of birth such as was not heretofore: for it was dead, having no motion. He, then, being pulled down . . . established this whole disposition of all things, being hanged up an image of the creation, wherein he made the things of the right hand into left hand and the left hand into right hand, and changed about all the marks of their nature, so that he thought those things that were not fair to be fair, and those things that were in truth evil, to be good. . . .
>
> And the figure wherein ye now see me hanging is the representation of that man that first came unto birth. ('Acts of Peter' 37)

It was held by the Church Fathers that, as Adam and Eve had disobeyed God at Satan's instigation, the human race had put themselves into Satan's power, so that the present world is under the Devil's dominion until Christ should finally conquer. This teaching is closely connected with what has been called the 'Ransom Interpretation of the Christian Revelation'. In this doctrine, it was stated that, as Satan had succeeded in his plan of temptation, and as humanity had succumbed to his deception, he justly held the human race in bondage. Jesus came to earth to be a ransom for the hostages. Only a human being who transcended flawed human nature was a sufficient ransom.

To explain how Jesus' coming released humanity from the Devil's dominion, some of the Fathers used the analogy of a trick played on him. The Devil was entitled to seize and punish sinful human beings, but when he tried to destroy a sinless being, he overstepped the bounds of justice, and so lost all his rights and had to free them. But even though he was thus defeated, the Devil still tries to thwart the plan of salvation, and will do so until the final reckoning. This last teaching was given by the Church Fathers to show that though we are now

*Crucifixion of St Peter*. Sebastian Bourdon.
The Courtauld Institute

freed from inevitable slavery to evil, the pomps and vanities of this world are still ruled by the Prince of Darkness, and, if we are attached to them, we will be under his governance.

These teachings concerning the Ransom Theory were taken by many to be a historical fact, and were to play a great part in medieval belief in the Devil and his powers. They are a clear example of how confusing the use of metaphor can be. There is a continuous problem of distinguishing between belief in the meaning of a doctrinal exposition and belief in the actual facts contained in the story used to explain it.

But however powerful the Devil may have seemed, his powers were always understood by the Church Fathers to be limited by God. According to Origen, the purpose of the world is to train us to return to our primal state, when we will be as we were meant to be. And both he and St Augustine envisaged God as using even the Devil's work to conform to this end. Temptations and trials are part of the training, and it has been said of Satan that no one worked harder for Job's sanctity, though no one could have wanted it less (Charles Journet, *The Meaning of Evil*). Without the aim of a final return, said Origen, there is no purpose in the universe; purposelessness is the hallmark of sin, and the Devil had chosen purposelessness.

It seems almost certain from their writings that the Church Fathers, basing their ideas on the wording of the Old and New Testaments, conceived of the Devil, not only as the symbol of evil or the personification of all the evil in mankind, but as a cosmic being who existed in the universe. The army of demons, which he controlled, also had actual existence. Such a conception of the world was to colour the thinking and the outlook in Europe of both learned and ignorant until relatively modern times.

A permanent obstacle to the understanding of past ages, which makes the writing of truly accurate history all but impossible, is the fact that people of different eras have, as it were, 'spectacles of their age' through which their world is viewed. They are more or less unaware of these 'spectacles', and in any case, they are unable to see round them. We have our own twentieth-century 'spectacles' through which we see our world, and we are unable to see through those of preceding ages. So it is difficult for us to comprehend how, at the time of St Augustine, for instance, men lived in a world that was peopled with good and bad spirits, who had power to influence them. We cannot now put ourselves in their place.

We are very conscious, and becoming increasingly so, of the evil that is in the world today. The word 'Devil' and the concept of 'Devil' enters into our language and continually crops up in our everyday speech and expressions. Because, since the Renaissance period we have become homo-centric rather than theo-centric in our thinking, our present-day 'spectacles' may possibly show us 'the Devil' entirely as the sum total of evil emanating from human beings, both individually and collectively, rather than as a malevolent spirit governing and directing evil forces which can be a danger to us. The conception of such a being is not part of modern thinking. People brought up and educated in a scientific and technological age simply cannot see the human struggle in those terms, although for centuries this is how it was seen.

Our scientific upbringing persuades us to look down on the ancient way of thinking, assuming that we know better. In a sense we are right, because the scientific knowledge which we possess today makes it impossible for us to see the physical world now as it was seen then. From what we now know about the physical nature of the universe and about the mechanism of our own bodies, we cannot view, for instance, natural calamities or our own diseases as the work of evil spirits, or caused by the machinations of a hostile intelligence. We are right in relation to the aspect of the world which *we* have been educated to see – the solely material aspect – but it is a different aspect from that which was seen by people in former times. We may not be so right in relation to that.

# CHAPTER 3

# The Three Spheres of the Devil and the Apportioning of Blame

From the Apocryphal Books and from Revelation, the Church Fathers developed their cosmological doctrines on the Devil. From the stories and sayings in the Gospels, they developed their teaching on his relation with individual Christians.

The language used in early Church teaching laid great stress on the need to do battle against the armies of Satan, and on the duty of Christians to support the armies of the Good Kingdom battling against the armies of the Bad. There was always the danger, and this danger continued, of regarding the two opposing forces as possessing equal and independent might; and it continued to be a problem for Christian theologians – how to lay stress on the great and dangerous power of Satan, and, at the same time, maintain the omnipotence of a merciful God.

The concept of the Devil has been used in theological writing to 'justify the ways of God to men' – what is called theodicy – 'the vindication of the Divine Providence, or government, in view of the existence of evil' (Leibnitz). The teachings of theodicy were given with the purpose of widening the scale of thought, and so making religious doctrines more understandable. People were encouraged to contemplate human life in relation to a Divine Plan, and not to think of it solely in terms of their own understanding of what was good or what was bad for themselves. But, though there has been, through the centuries, continual debate concerning the conception of evil on a cosmological scale, this is not its most important theological aspect.

The story of Lucifer, the Fallen Angel, as a part of theodicy, gave to the concept of the Devil a cosmic form. But we can have no actual knowledge of an evil force on so great a scale, and we can have no true idea of what is good or harmful on such a scale. Only in relation to human beings in our world does the concept of an Evil Force have any practical meaning for our minds, and, if we do not make clear on what scale we are thinking, much confusion results.

There can be said to be three levels on which the concept of the Devil has been used. The first could be to explain the introduction, on a cosmological scale, of what appears to us to be imperfection and contradiction in the universe. The second could be the description of the evil forces and influences that seem to have surrounded humankind from the beginning. This is on a smaller scale, the human scale, but still taken on a universal level. The third could be the concept of the Devil as he has been understood by human beings in their own individual experience, and in that of their fellows, when they are conscious of fierce temptation and harmful suggestion.

It never seems to have been suggested in any doctrine concerning the Evil One that there are three Devils, in three spheres, one subservient to another. But it may be necessary to keep the spheres separate in one's mind when using the term 'Devil', in whatever form it is understood. Throughout the history of the concept of the Devil and of the varying stages of belief in him, the three spheres have tended to intermingle.

The belief that there is an evil to be resisted has been accepted from time immemorial; and the idea of an active power of evil, embodying the forces of darkness, is an idea that has persisted through the ages. It is only in relatively modern times that the actual existence of a cosmic power, hostile to good and embodying a permanent hatred of humanity, has been generally questioned. But the fact remains that most human beings still feel that there are definite evils existing in our world, from wherever they are thought to come. There is still a sense of opposition between what is supposed to be good and what is thought to be harmful, in our own communities, if not in the universe. This may be regarded as the second sphere of the Devil – the Devil in relation to humankind and its varied activities on earth.

Despite the idea of an opposition between 'progress and

regress' in our world, moral teachings as to what is good and right and what is bad and wrong differ in various times and places. For instance, in twelfth-century Spain it would have been considered deeply immoral not to avenge an insult to one's family by killing the insulter; and again, at the time of the Maccabees, in the Judaea of the second century BC, the eating of pork was such a heinous offence that an ignominious death was thought preferable. But a general understanding, independent of any specific moral codes, that there is a 'good' in human conduct and that there is a 'bad', distinct from what is immediately desirable or undesirable, is found in all cultures and civilisations, and seems to be central to any form of civilised life.

People often talk about natural calamities as great evils. But they are not thought of as evil in the same way as the evil committed by human beings, although even here a moral sense is often included. In ancient times great disasters and plagues were considered to be the Devil's work, brought about either for purposes of testing or for punishment, or merely because the Devil was given a certain amount of power over sinful human beings. Today we do not connect these events with a good or evil force, although sometimes there is a feeling of moral blame towards a Creator who could have allowed such things to occur; alternatively, it may be thought that great goodness and heroism can come out of these disasters, and that therefore they have a purpose. But, in whatever way they are now considered, we do not feel that it is here that we have to face the Evil One in fact or in metaphor.

The age-old idea of a cosmic battle between good and evil has sometimes been conceived in popular imagination as a battle between the angelic forces and the hosts of Satan. Out of this conception has arisen, in various forms, the notion that human beings, themselves, have little part to play in the drama.

The Old Testament and Apocalyptic writers, and later, the Church Fathers, expounded their doctrine of the Fallen Angel who became the Devil in order to explain the metaphysical concept of struggle in the universe. This idea of cosmic opposition to a Divine Plan often became confused with the idea of the evil which seems to lie within humanity. The ever-continuing desire of human beings to avoid taking upon themselves the responsibility for their bad actions led to a growing belief that Satan brought sin into the world, and, as Tempter, is responsible for the weaknesses in human beings. Therefore it is he who causes us to sin.

In the Jewish Wisdom literature, Jesus Sirach, as early as the second century BC, wrote to counteract this tendency of sinful men to blame the Devil: 'When the fool curseth his adversary [Satan], he curseth his own soul.' And he said that every man is his own Satan – his own adversary. The Book of Enoch, also, placing responsibility for wrong doing firmly on individual Man, says: 'No sin has been sent on earth, but Man, himself, has created it.' St Augustine, in the fifth century, insisted that Man's will brings the evil. It does not come from outside.

In the present day, blame for one's wrongdoing is unlikely to be placed on a being termed 'the Devil'. Whatever conception has been held of the Devil in the past, he has always been understood, in orthodox Christian teaching, to act through human beings. And in the teaching that came to Christendom through the Church Fathers, it was firmly accepted that the Devil could not force anyone to sin. It was taught that freedom of choice, however limited, was granted to human beings, and therefore they could choose whether or not to follow the Devil's suggestions. This was often emphasised by spiritual writers in the past, so that sinful men and women should not excuse themselves from their errors, by putting all the blame on the Tempter.

Nowadays, the word 'Devil' is most often used as a mere figure of speech, and the misdeeds of individuals are more likely to be blamed on society than on diabolic inspiration. The dictionary definition of 'society' is 'the aggregate of persons living together in a more or less ordered community'. Nobody has ever seen 'society', because such abstractions do not actually exist. Social ills come, therefore, through the actions of the people who compose 'society'. Each individual's life may well be shaped by factors of geography, of economics, of caste systems, of customs; and each individual may be part of a group or community who share many opinions and feelings. But thoughts, emotions and actions come only from individuals and are their sole responsibility. There is no avoiding it. Whether evil influences are said to come through 'the Devil, the Prince of Darkness', or through the modern devil, 'Society', harmful thoughts, words and actions can only manifest through individual human beings, whatever influence may be acting on them.

We, as individual beings, however contradictory we may be, can be strongly influenced by each other. Human minds together can create a 'climate of opinion', beneficial or harmful; human emotions together can be destructive or constructive – they can fuel mob violence, or they can be channelled into a collective prayer for peace.

A man, swayed by the emotions of a mob, may do things which he would never do of his own volition, but still the mob is composed of human beings, and it is still up to the individual to allow himself to be part of it or not. It is often held by psychologists today that much that we find evil may come from subconscious tendencies, manifesting through collective minds, and it is of this, they say, that the so-called 'Devil' consists. But whether the evil found to be within humanity has become personified as 'the Devil', or whether, as has been believed throughout the ages and in innumerable countries, there is an actual evil Enemy who persuades men to these thoughts and emotions, each person is able, though sometimes surrounded by very great obstacles, to choose under what influence to place himself; and however these evil forces are described, they can only act through individual human beings.

In whatever way we think of the Devil, he can only be conceived in connection with humanity. It makes no sense to talk of the Devil tempting a cow or a crocodile. This, again, must be because the human being is considered to have a power of choice; a human being can choose under which influence to place himself, whereas an animal cannot. The battlefield is within the human mind and heart. And it is at this point that the crucial question always arises: is the Devil purely a product of the human mind and heart or has he an independent existence of his own?

Great thinkers of the past in different cultures and religions have written of the Devil as existing both as a metaphor and as a being with objective existence. This seems to be of the utmost importance in their writings about him. Clement of Alexandria, in the second century, wrote that he exists both inside the human mind and outside it. We do not know what Satan is objectively: he is – and he is not. But, he said, we can know how he (whatever he is) seems to act in our minds. We can know that evil thoughts, whether they *are* Satan or whether they are caused by a being called Satan, come from an evil principle and separate us from all goodness (cf. J. B. Russell, *Satan, The Devil and the Church Fathers*).

In the twelfth century, Al Ghazali, a mystical theologian of the Muslim religion, wrote that, men's minds being limited, God was obliged to speak to them in metaphor, and this He did in the Koran, which otherwise we would not be able to understand. Thus God, in the Koran, used Satan as a metaphor, though we can also understand Satan's works through our own experience. In the Koran, there is the story of how Satan refused to bow down before the newly created Adam, though he was commanded by God so to do. This we are to understand as a metaphor for pride and for the refusal of our passions to bow before reason. Satan, or Eblis, as he is also called, is here the personification of obstacles blocking us from God. But this does not mean, Al Ghazali writes, that Satan *is* just a metaphor – only that we dare not ascribe ultimate reality to our conception of him. The 'personality' that we give him may not be at all what is in the mind of God. So that, on whatever scale the conception of the Devil is taken, Al Ghazali conceives it as dangerous to our thinking to treat him as other than metaphor – whether a metaphor for a cosmic force in the universe or for our own evil inclinations: objective knowledge is beyond us (cf. J. B. Russell, *Lucifer, The Devil in the Middle Ages*).

The religion of Islam was much influenced by the Old and New Testaments in its description of the Devil. The Koran tells how Eblis, having been dismissed from Heaven because of his pride and disobedience, asked to be allowed respite to tempt men until the day of Resurrection. 'He said to God, "I will seduce all except thy chosen servants." God said, "Verily, you will have no power on my servants" ' (Suras 17 and 38).

So, common to both the Christian and Islamic religions, is the teaching that if a human being is a servant of God – that is, if he attains a certain level of being within himself, the Kingdom of God within – the Devil, when he attacks, will find him beyond his domain. 'The Devil is a chained dog who can bark and worry, but he cannot bite if we keep out of his reach' (St Augustine, quoted by John Nicholas Grou, eighteenth-century priest, in *Spiritual Maxims*).

In the same way, the objective existence of a malevolent spirit may have been part of the doctrine of the first Church Fathers, but of greater importance for them was their teaching that the struggle took place in the human mind. It was the responsibility of each individual human being to resist attack and keep out of the Devil's reach. Their teaching was centred on the third sphere of the Devil, that of the individual.

From the Gospel sayings about the Devil, from what was written in the Epistles, from teachings in the Jewish scriptures, the Church Fathers developed the Church's doctrine on the Evil One. They lived in an age when people had for generations been accustomed to envisage their sinful urges and temptations as attacks by a hostile spirit, so that the description of evil in personalised form would come naturally to them.

Many people now feel that there are evil influences in the world on a large scale; and, on a personal level, most people, at some time in their lives, have been conscious of a fierce inner struggle against thoughts and desires that they knew to be harmful. Probably the majority of people in the West would be unwilling to ascribe either the evil influence or the harmful suggestions to the work of a being called 'the Devil'. It may be true to say that, though, in religious writings and even in general conversation, the Devil is often said to be the instigator of these evils, very few people actively envisage such a being. Our 'spectacles', for better or for worse, are too firmly fixed.

But however the focal point of evil is understood, it seems that, through all the ages, human beings have been loth to blame themselves for their own misdeeds. It has seemed natural for them to hold the conviction 'that the causes of all their manifestations, both good and bad, are not they themselves personally nor their own criminal essence-egoism, but some or other external foreign influences not depending on them at all' (G. Gurdjieff, *All and Everything, Beelzebub's Tales to His Grandson*). In the past, the Devil could be blamed; now, though the Prince of Darkness may be ignored, blame is still placed upon some external factor – on our genes, on our upbringing, on society.

In earlier times, when the idea of the Devil occupied an important place in people's minds, those who were struggling to put Christian teachings, as they understood them, into practice, took St Augustine's precepts very seriously. Men and women committed to the religious life conceived the fight against temptation as a struggle to rise above the Devil's sphere to where he had no power. They certainly considered themselves personally responsible for the outcome of any evil suggestion. But, for them, the Prince of Darkness was felt to have a very real existence, as tempter and seducer, both within and without. It is again that question of the 'within and without' which creates the Devil's mystery.

# CHAPTER 4

# The Positive and the Negative Devil: From the Desert Fathers to the Scholastics

Some of the clearest examples of how inner struggle with temptation was conceived in times past are found in the lives of the Desert Fathers.

In the fourth century, soon after the recognition of Christianity by Constantine, many Christians abandoned what they now considered to be too easy a life, and fled to the desert. They held that true Christianity involved hardship and danger, such as had been endured during the times of persecution, but which now no longer existed. In the desert they had to meet dangers of another sort. In their lonely life of prayer and ascetic practice, they came face to face with 'the Devil' – the temptation to thoughts, emotions and desires opposed to their spiritual aim. They had to face the terrible attacks of 'Accidié' – the 'noon-day devil' of sloth and boredom – who made the monk see his life as pointless, and time to be dragging endlessly on, with no hope of alleviation. And, in the monk's life of solitude and hardship, there were probably many other dangers unknown to people in ordinary life.

Stories of the lives of the Desert Monks and collections of their sayings were circulated, copied in monasteries and much read by succeeding generations. The most famous of these were *The Life of St Anthony*, by St Athanasius, and *The Paradise of the Fathers*, by Bishop Palladius. In these books

*Temptation of
St Anthony the Hermit.*
Florentine Woodcut.
Warburg Instute

were stories of furious physical battles with the Devil, which the Desert Monks had to endure. There were also descriptions of the fierce blows and wounds suffered by the great St Anthony in his encounters with the Evil One. All these tales had a powerful influence on the way in which the Devil was then conceived. The monks took the place of the martyrs, as heroes and 'athletes of God'; the desert monk was held to be a warrior fighting against the might of the Devil. And so the Devil was increasingly feared.

In these manuscripts, the Devil and the demons who appeared to the Desert Fathers were always given a literal interpretation. It is impossible to be certain what interpretation the Fathers themselves gave to them. The outlook of the time in which they lived would accustom them to the thought of an evil spirit waiting nearby, ready to attack. A person's spiritual experience or inward vision is liable to be given visual representation in accordance with the religious tradition in which he lives. This does not mean that all visions are figments of the imagination. A human mind can only use material that belongs to it, and if such supranormal experiences take place, they are likely to be clothed in the imagery to which the mind is accustomed. So, to the monks of the desert, however they understood him, the Devil was very real indeed.

It had been generally accepted from the earliest times that the Devil would fight much harder for the soul of a very good man than he would for that of an ordinary sinner. The struggle of a desert monk, therefore, against the Devil's wiles was likely to be an intense one. This is understandable: the greater the effort, the greater the temptation. The stories of the Desert Fathers gave further impetus to the idea of the world as a battleground, where the Devil was fighting to gain possession of men's souls.

Pope Gregory the Great, in the sixth century, was vigorous in expressing the idea of a continuous battle with the Enemy. It was largely due to his powerful influence that the conception of the world as a battlefield became a part of the general outlook of the time. If we lose our attention for a moment, he said, the Devil's army swarms in. The Devil attacks by blurring our understanding, by deceiving our judgement, or by inducing despair. All sins come through the work of the Devil, but no temptation is allowed by God without our being given the ability to resist.

This doctrine that God both permits and restricts evil formed part of Pope Gregory's firm stand against dualism, the belief that there are two independent and equal forces in the universe – that of good and that of evil. The acceptance of this dualism had always been considered a danger to the correct development of Christian doctrine. Judaism had come under the influence of Persian Zoroastrianism, which took shape as an avowedly dualistic religion. But, for Judaism and for Christianity, as strictly monotheistic religions, it was essential to maintain that there was one omnipotent God. There could not be two independent opposing forces.

The dualism in Greek philosophy – the opposition between spirit and matter, and between the higher and the lower world – also had a pervasive influence on religious thinkers in the first centuries of Christianity. Many Gnostic sects, for instance, regarded the material world as a prison. They believed that sparks of the eternal spiritual light had been imprisoned within the matter of our world. From this conception came the idea of permanent hostility between matter and spirit. Separation of the spiritual from the corporeal, freeing the spirit from the bondage of the flesh, was understood by the Gnostics to be the aim of the religious life. The world of matter was thus considered to be entirely evil, and, in some of the Gnostic schools, the Old Testament God, who had created our material world, was equated with the Devil, and was the enemy of the loving God of Spirit. They held that, in our world, good and evil powers were at war, and the 'world, the flesh and the Devil' were one and the same.

The dualism in Manicheism, the powerful religious system that spread eastward from Persia in the third century, was yet more emphatic. The good and evil powers were held to be co-eternal and equal, uncreated and infinite. In the Manichean belief, there were two rulers in the universe, and two kingdoms. There was a kingdom of light and a kingdom of darkness, opposed to each other for all eternity. Out of the kingdom of darkness Satan and the demons were born. According to the Manichean myth, God created Primal Man – the original ideal pattern of Man – to fight against Satan. Satan overcame Primal Man, and robbed him of some particles of light. These he mixed with five elements of the dark world. Out of these mixed elements, God formed our world, in order to deliver the imprisoned light.

Satan, the supreme ruler of the dark kingdom, was identified with matter. The good power was light, clarity: the evil power, darkness, repressed desire. The ruler of the dark kingdom represented the carnal condition of Man. He was the embodiment of evil, because he was supremely irrational, without reason and devoid of all that was spiritual; in fact, he was the Lord of Primordial Chaos.

As the Manichees took part in the religious observances of the various peoples among whom they lived, the Manichean Prince of Darkness, ruler of the Dark Kingdom, became closely associated with the Christian idea of the Devil. In most Gnostic systems, and certainly in Manicheism, the Devil was the embodiment of the dark forces of ignorance and materiality, which for ever bar the return of the spirit to its source.

Dualist tendencies continued to enter Christian thinking, and the Council of Braga was called in 563 especially to deny this dualism, which implied two separate and opposing independent worlds – one of spirit and light, and the other of matter and darkness. Under the influence of the Manichean doctrines, many Christians began to believe that Lucifer, the Devil, had created the world of matter, and, like the Manichees, believed that everything material was evil. In these beliefs, the Devil was held to be an evil being totally independent of God. The Council laid down that the Devil had been created by God and fell through the exercise of the free will which had been given him. This was to show that there was one all-powerful God, not two independent, opposing principles. Pope Gregory affirmed that the Devil was prince of this world, not because he was lord of Matter, but because he was lord of sinful humans.

Teachings on the Devil were becoming increasingly consistent and definite, but there were many dangers in them. In Pope Gregory's doctrine, which followed that of St Augustine, one part of our world was Christ's – the world of the just; the other Lucifer's. It then became the accepted opinion that under Lucifer's governance, as well as all sinful Christians, belonged pagans, heretics and Jews. It is clear where this was likely to lead.

The 'Ransom' conception of Christianity, which had been expounded by many of the Church Fathers, occupied such an important place in people's minds that it increasingly coloured the ordinary citizens' view of their religion. For centuries, many people thought of this world as under the dominion of Satan. They understood that, as a result of the Fall of Man, our world had, with complete justice, become Satan's property. Justice, in earlier times was not so much equated with fairness and equality, as it is now, as with the idea of the correct order of everything in the world and in the universe. Because the Devil had just rights in this world, people, therefore, saw themselves as in constant danger from him. Christ had ransomed us, it was true, but the Devil was still allowed to attack sinners who strayed from the side of Christ. This he could do until he was finally overthrown by the Hosts of Heaven at the end of the world. This general understanding of Christianity was one of the major reasons why the Devil played such a powerful part in the life of the Middle Ages.

The Scholastic theologians of the eleventh and twelfth centuries continued to question the extent of Satan's powers and his whole position in the plan of the universe. They debated the cause and origin of his fall – whether it took place through pride or through envy – and endlessly discussed whether the fall of angels came before or after the creation of Man. Yet, strangely enough, the 'Ransom' conception of Christianity was becoming less important in the exposition of Christian dogma.

What was called the 'Sacrifice Theory of Salvation' was made more central to Church teaching and to the works of theologians. St Anselm, in the eleventh century, insisted that what we owe is to God, and should not be thought of as owed to the Devil. He said that we could not, of ourselves, offer sufficient sacrifice to restore our distorted humanity; this could only be done by God-made-Man. In the light of this conception, the Devil's role in the human story was made less significant. By the end of the thirteenth century, the 'Ransom Theory' had all but disappeared from theological writings. Therefore, although for the ordinary people of the time the Devil was still of prime importance and often held the centre of the stage in their lives, for theologians he began to play a much smaller part in the way Christian doctrines were expressed.

Scholastic theologians were struggling to define the meaning of 'evil'. In the same way as the Christian writers of the fourth century, and in the same way as St Augustine, they thought of evil in Platonic terms, as being a privation of good.

Evil was thought not to exist in itself, but to consist of mere lack of being.

St Anselm, wrote a treatise on the nature of evil, 'The Fall of the Devil'. He said that as the word 'nothing' refers only to what it negates, so the word 'evil' refers only to the good it negates. Blindness is lack of sight; war is lack of peace. The lack, which 'evil' is, becomes a 'something' only in speech; but lack of goodness produces its disastrous effects. No one wills evil, as evil is nothing in itself. But a lesser good can be willed. The Devil willed the good of his own happiness instead of the justice of God's Cosmos. Human beings can also choose to reject God's pattern and bring disharmony and alienation into the world in the same way as had the Devil. Choosing illusory good is the worst sin, the sin which the Devil tempted Adam and Eve to commit.

Later, St Thomas Aquinas developed these ideas. Evil can only exist in something good; it is a pulling away from a natural movement towards God: 'Evil is a given subject's failure to reach its full actuality.' It is, in fact, the privation of a good which ought to be there.

As a modern writer has explained, 'evil' being called a privation does not mean that it is non-existent. Blindness does not strictly mean 'absence of sight', but 'absence of sight from where it ought to be' (Charles Journet, *The Meaning of Evil*). The absence, the lack of something where something should be, can cause catastrophe, as can its corollary, the existence of something where it should not be, again negating right order: 'But when you shall see the abomination of desolation standing where it ought not (let him that readeth understand), then let them that be in Judaea flee to the mountains' (Mark 13:14).

In this 'privation' theology of evil, in which evil is described as the negation of goodness, it might seem that 'the Devil', taken as the focal point of all evil, is entirely nebulous and feeble. But in the ancient Babylonian myth, Tiamat, the Dragon, fighting to reduce the universe to primordial chaos, is far from feeble. Chaos, the lack or absence of order, has long been held to 'belong to the Devil'. On the human scale, 'The Devil is the absence of all that is highest and most purified in human beings; absence of religious feeling, absence of vision, absence of the feeling for beauty, absence of awareness of the miraculous' (P. D. Ouspensky, *Talks with a Devil*). What we call 'the Devil' may then be a destructive force in the universe, which, when it comes into contact with Man, can eliminate the good in him: 'This non-existence, like a vacuum sucks creatures into the void of non-being' (Dyonisius the Areopagite, Christian writer of the early sixth century).

Whether this lack, this negation, which is how 'evil' has been described, *is* the Devil, or whether it is caused by him, has importance only in trying to discover what we mean by the possible *existence* of Satan: is there, in existence, a disembodied intelligence, hostile to humanity? Doubt of his reality or unreality has caused him to be described as 'ambiguity incarnate' (Introduction by Charles Moeller to *Satan Etudes Carmelitaines*, edited by George D. Smith) – 'The Devil is the Prince of *Darkness*, the caricature of God, and can never become incarnate save by an ontological "absence"; he can only act via the man who lets himself be carried in his wake.' This is where habitual metaphorical use of the term 'Devil' causes so many difficulties in thinking about him. He may be given a personality, a meaning, as the distortion that is in a man; or perhaps it is better to say, that because of the emptiness within, the Devil enters – there is nothing to stop him, the man can be blown first this way and then that. But this emptiness is the obverse of the emptiness described and desired by saints of all religions. It is an absence, an emptiness of reality; in fact, a lack of true order, which means a distortion – an upside-down vision of the universe, and the province of the Father of Lies.

Thomas Aquinas, like Augustine and many other Christian theologians, was strongly influenced by the ideas of the Neoplatonists. They held that, from God, the All-Perfect Being, came all things – angels, humans, animals, plants, inanimate objects, unformed matter. Each step down was a further step from God, therefore less spiritual, less real, and having less being. The Jewish theosophical system, which claimed to have been transmitted uninterruptedly from prophets and patriarchs since the creation of the first man, and known from the eleventh and twelfth centuries as the Cabbala, used a similar idea in its cosmology, though with a different emphasis. As in the many Gnostic systems, the Cabbala stated that the universe was produced by a series of emanations from the infinite, unknown God, here termed the Ain Soph. The first ten emanations, the Sephiroth, each a triad, produced the next ten, until four worlds were created.

Each world, being further removed from the primordial source, became ever coarser and less spiritual. The fourth world was known as the World of Action or World of Matter, where all was subject to change and corruption. Man was formed to inhabit this world as a microcosm of the universe. His soul's destiny, after its probation on the earth, was to return to the infinite source of its being. Creation involves limitation, and this creation, with its necessary imperfection, could not come direct from the Ain Soph, but had to be evolved through the medium of the Sephiroth, the intelligences which emanated from the Ain Soph as rays from a luminary. So the cosmos was formed by multiplication and descent.

Thus, in both the Neoplatonic and the later Cabbalistic system of ideas, there is the conception of a descent. This descent inevitably implies some form of imperfection in the universe. Anything that is not God must lack perfection, and if anything is to grow towards perfection it must be imperfect as it is. So St Thomas Aquinas wrote, 'Evil is the price to be paid for a non-static cosmos.'

A non-static cosmos implies struggle. No living thing can exist without struggle. In order not only to grow, but even to continue to live, there must be struggle; and there has to be opposition to be overcome, or no development is possible. And this applies to plants, animals and humans. The Neoplatonists conceived of imperfection increasing as creation expanded into greater materiality and into a greater distance from consciousness. Imperfection in nature does not seem to be at all the same thing as spiritual imperfection in human beings. Nevertheless, the idea shows that mankind, as part of a non-static universe, is bound to contain within it the possibility of error and failure. 'Original Sin' was said by St Anselm to be so-called because it exists at the origin of each person. John Scotus Eruigena, John the Scot, in the ninth century, had written that Original Sin, or alienation from God, did not belong to our natural state (how we were meant to be) but to our existential state: from our birth we cling to illusory treasure, to what is not. The beginning of alienation and evil existed from the first moment of the cosmos. Because the cosmos was living and growing, there had to be a flaw in it.

There is a saying of Muhammad that 'God is a hidden treasure, and desires to be known'; therefore He created. Creation means the coming into being of something other than

God. Adam, through listening to the temptation of Satan, separated himself from God, so that mankind had to make its long journey through the world to reunite itself with Him. In this way, God's purpose in creation would finally be fulfilled.

The story in the Koran of Eblis refusing to bow before the newly created Adam, and so being banished from Heaven, has been understood by certain Sufi mystics to signify the necessity of what we term 'evil' in the Divine Plan of the universe. In their analogy, they speak of Eblis as fulfilling God's Will, since his refusal and fall was essential for the struggle and growth of the world. This interpretation of the myth of the Fall of Angels concentrates on the unity of God – that everything, both what seems good and what seems bad, is contained in Him. It is an interpretation that is totally non-dualistic. Nevertheless, the necessity of struggle is central to it.

In the life of humanity, there can be no goodness without some struggle with the bad. A being who had no possibility of making a wrong choice would be an automaton, not a human being. If there is any kind of free will for human beings, there has to be the freedom to fall. No person can be good who has nothing to overcome and has overcome nothing. Thus the Christian writers, also, held the Devil to have an important function. Like St Augustine, St Thomas Aquinas writes of God using even the Devil to create ultimate good. The cosmos, our world and the individual human being may each be seen as a battlefield. But, for the religious mind, the battle is fought for a purpose, and so the opposition has its role to play and should be recognised.

It is clear that, in our language, 'bad' can only be the contrast of 'good', and, in our world, we cannot think of 'bad' without comparing it with 'good'. So it would seem that it is impossible to believe in the Devil without believing in God, since a totally 'bad' universe under the complete power of a totally 'bad' being is inconceivable. This might be another reason for the Devil, if he exists, to persuade us that he does not.

# CHAPTER 5

# The Appearance of the Devil and the Abode of Hell

It was inevitable that those who lived when belief in the Devil was strong and held a central place in everyday life would tend to give him a form in their mind's eye. As with all abstractions, it is easier to grasp the idea of a focal point of evil if it is personified. The Church Fathers, from the earliest times, insisted that the Evil One and his army of demons were of the nature of spirit, and this continued to be emphasised by Christian theologians. But in the first century AD it was also allowed by Christian writers that the Devil, though a spirit, could take on any form that he chose, in order to tempt and harm mankind.

A physical appearance was never given to Satan in the writings of the Old or the New Testaments. The nearest approach to the idea that he could assume a visual form was the literal interpretation given to St Paul's teaching that, in order to deceive, even Satan could transform himself into an angel of light (2 Corinthians 11:14). The idea that the Evil One could take any shape at will was also strengthened by the equation of Satan with the serpent who tempted Adam and Eve. So the Devil's power to manifest in bodily form was connected, in early days, with the purpose of deception rather than, as in later times, with the aim of producing terror. Nevertheless, the descriptions of the Dragon in Revelation gave a picture of the Evil One as a frightful monster, and this made a powerful and lasting impression on popular imagination.

Nowhere in the Gospels themselves is there any suggestion

at all of evil spirits taking visible shape, and there is no mention of the story of the Garden of Eden nor of the War in Heaven. Nevertheless, even the greatest Christian thinkers and spiritual writers of past ages envisaged the possibility of evil spirits assuming a form, since it was inevitable that even profound thinkers viewed their world through 'the spectacles of their age'.

St Augustine wrote that the demons might have aerial bodies, and, having been thrust out of Heaven, might inhabit the atmosphere around our world. So there were times when it was a general belief that the air was full of spirits ready to harm us. But, characteristically, St Augustine said that this belief had no importance either way – watchfulness was all. St Augustine, also, when writing *The City of God*, took for granted that the educated pagans who read it would naturally believe in the existence of demons, for he said that it was foolish of them to fear these creatures; it is what demons suggest to our minds that is important, not they themselves.

The Church fathers used the texts available to them to develop their interpretation of the Christian Revelation. They understood the New Testament to be a fulfilment, not an abrogation of the Old, so Old Testament teachings and imagery were naturally used by them in the elaboration of Christian doctrines. It would have been as unthinkable for them not to base all their deductions and their teachings about the universe on the actual words of the Scriptures as it would be for most people nowadays to hold a world-view divorced from scientific discovery. And if these words existed in Scripture, having the meanings normally given to them at that period of time, then what was stated there could be taken as the literal truth. However, the various forms assumed by the demonic beings described in the stories of struggle with evil often came from other sources than the Old and New Testaments; and the traditional form of the Devil himself, which has come down to us through centuries of art and literature, has also had a diverse history.

No iconography or portrayal of the Devil in painting or carving has been found dating from before the sixth century, and not very much has been found before the ninth. After that, the number of representations of him increased rapidly. But from earlier writings, we know how he was generally imagined. He was frequently said to take animal form; for

*The Devil Pointing out Hidden Treasure*. From Seligman's
'Mirror of Magic'.

instance, he was pictured in the form of the wily serpent; and, following St Peter's metaphor of 'a roaring lion', was said to take the shape of that fiercest of animals. But the gods of the pagans contributed most to the visual conception of the Evil One. It was a widely held view, in the first Christian centuries, that pagan gods were servants of the Devil, and pagan rites of worship were the Devil's parodies of Christian sacraments. And so the pagan deities, particularly those of Greece, were very much associated with the Devil, and it is largely from them that his traditional portraits have come.

It would be unusual to find an educated person today, whatever his conception of the Devil might be, who believes that he could one day meet a being featured like the Evil One as portrayed in Western art. But the fact that the Devil has this portrait may explain many of the qualities that have been attributed to him. The history of his visual representation is part of the history of his concept.

The picture of the Devil that we are most accustomed to see is that of a shaggy, goat-like creature, with horns and tail. The goat might be considered to be a useful animal, but the simile of 'goats and sheep' had been used in the New Testament to differentiate the faithful followers of Christ from the unfaithful. So there were already unpleasant associations belonging to the goat when he was found to be connected with the deities worshipped by pagans. It was primarily from these deities that the Devil got his traditional form and attributes; and, from among them, the greatest influence came from the Greek god, Pan.

The fact that the Christians had to make their way in a pagan world, that pagan Rome had persecuted them and that it was by changing the beliefs of pagans that the Christian religion could hold its own made it natural for the first Christians to connect pagan deities with the Evil One. Strangely enough, it was the Manichean tendencies within Christianity, tendencies which have never quite disappeared, that contributed to the Devil's appearance. For the dualist conception that matter was evil, in contrast with the goodness of spirit, still invaded Christian thought and the general Christian outlook. It was believed that the fleshly body imprisoned the spirit, and so was said to be the work of cosmic evil. Theological statements were made to counteract this type of thinking, but it persisted on all levels. Consequently, the numerous pagan gods associated with fertility and reproduction, and therefore with the most carnal aspect of life, were thought to be especially connected with the Devil. Sexuality was the Devil's domain, not only because sexual temptations were among the most powerful, but because earthiness and materiality belonged to him. Therefore, it was not surprising that Pan, the most earthy of all the gods, should seem to be the nearest personification of the Prince of Darkness.

In Greek mythology, Pan was the son of Hermes, and was born with horns and a tail, a goat's beard and hooves, and covered with hair. He was a rustic god, sacred to woods and fields, and with him, in the forests were the Panisci, the forest imps, his sons and daughters, who terrified human beings with evil dreams and apparitions. The cult of Pan was widespread in Greece by the third century BC, and through a possible misinterpretation of his name, he began to be worshipped as a universal god. As a god of nature, he possessed powers of inspiration and prophecy. But especially he represented sexual desire, the force of destruction and creation. In Christian eyes, he became connected with everything that was evil. To increase his evil reputation, he was believed, in Greek mythology, to be among the companions of Dionysus, the god of fruitfulness, symbolised by the vine. The Dionysian myth, personifying nature's cycle of death and renewed life, mortification and ecstasy, became a cult with wild and terrifying rites, famous for the drunken orgies of its followers. Tales of such happenings became the pattern for later conceptions of witches' sabbaths.

The goat was also sacred to Dionysus, as a symbol of reproduction – his horns, a sign of fertility and power. The goat-shape of Pan was thus doubly devilish, and the goat's cloven hoof was to become the Devil's most famous attribute. So Pan, with his troop of forest imps resembling demons, represented a pagan power over everything carnal and earthly. This gave to those trying to create a pictorial image for the Evil One whom they feared, a shape that seemed to encompass all his wickedness. To the Christians, Pan seemed to be the epitome of the heathen gods. He represented excess and debauchery, the vices of the world of matter, and so was the embodiment of paganism.

Tertullian and some of the early Christian writers had spoken of heathens as part of the Devil's army, therefore it was generally understood that to fight paganism was to fight against the Devil on the side of Christ. Paganism had to be destroyed.

There was a certain story current in the first century which had been told by Plutarch. Plutarch was not himself a Christian; indeed he was priest and archon of the Pythian Apollo. But the story, for the Christians, came to illustrate the triumph of Christianity over the pagan gods. Plutarch had written a dialogue, *On the Cessation of Oracles*, which discussed the question whether there are intermediate spirits who communicate the will of the gods to men, and he tried to give reasons why divine inspiration seemed to have been withdrawn from the ancient centres of prophecy. The legend he relates appears in this dialogue.

The story tells of the pilot, Thamus, who was sailing by the island of Paxi, in the time of the Emperor Tiberius. As his ship sailed by, he heard a mighty voice echoing from the dark woods. The voice cried out, 'Make this proclamation to the world: Pan is dead, Great Pan is dead.' The time of the story was said to coincide with the time of the Crucifixion of Christ, and so, to the Christians, the story heralded the death of the old world and the beginning of the new.

Pan was dead, but the Devil lived on in his disguise. The grinning, goat-like, hairy Devil became the recognised portrait of the Evil One. But it was also known of the Devil that he had once been a great angel. So the wings of an angel belonged to him. But the beautiful feathered wings of a bird, soaring into the heavens, could not be associated with an ugly creature of the dark. Though the Devil kept his wings, they were stripped of their heavenly plumage and became the great black, leathery wings of a giant bat. This sinister being could well be used by preachers and prophets as a dire warning to those who were tempted to stray from the right path.

The visualised image of the Devil was ever present in people's minds. This is one of the factors which causes the life of the Middle Ages to appear so different from our own, making it almost impossible for us to imagine ourselves in that time and with the outlook of that time. The fear engendered by belief in a Satanic enemy led often to disaster, and even to the distortion of the very meaning of the Christian religion. Yet it may have induced a realisation of the need for inner watchfulness, which is absent today, and a feeling of purpose which the sense of battle brings. But the superstitions which flourished could do nothing but harm. It was probably exceedingly difficult, during those times, to disentangle an intelligent fear of evil from the fear of the monstrous beings which were conjured out of men's minds.

The Prince of Darkness was seen as the ruler of the Kingdom of Hell, and his aim and pleasure was, therefore, to drag human souls down to his nether kingdom, where he could oversee their punishments. In the New Testament, there is no word of the Devil being responsible for punishing sinners in Hell. It is not quite clear how this belief grew up. It may have come from the long-held belief that Satan had been allowed a limited power to tempt and test souls; and there was very probably a connection with the verse in Revelation which tells of the star falling from Heaven and being given the key of the bottomless pit (Revelation 9:1). Certainly, pictures of the Devil carrying lost souls to Hell abound in medieval art. The Devil's pitchfork, which may have derived from Neptune's trident – a symbol of power over earth and sea – became seen as an instrument of torture for the damned.

The idea of the Devil ruling over a place of punishment was a relatively late one. The Ransom Interpretation of Christianity gave credence to the conception of the Devil presiding over Hell and being forced to release the sinless Christ. The third-century Apocryphal Gospel of Nicodemus tells the story of Christ descending into Hell to set free the just souls imprisoned there by Satan. As, in this story, there were righteous souls in Satan's kingdom, the word, 'Hell' cannot here have had its usual connotation with eternal punishment. It must have meant merely the habitation of the dead, and Satan presiding there may have been equated with Pluto, the Greek pantheon's ruler of the Underworld. Death was closely connected with Satan, and the Underworld with the Prince of Darkness.

The early Hebrew word for 'Hell', 'Sheol', also had a neutral meaning. Like the Greek 'Hades', it described the abode of departed spirits, who went there after death, whether their lives had been just or unjust. There, in a dim and shadowy form, they were said to exist. This was the popular understanding in early biblical times. The Jewish prophets and writers of the post-exilic era gave a stronger meaning to the word 'Hell'. The idea of retribution and punishment was included in it. In the time of the Apocryphal Gospels, the place of punishment had become 'Gehenna', the torment of fire and brimstone for the wicked. All these expressions could be understood in many ways, and all were often taken completely literally, both in this period and in later ages. They lent unspeakable terror to the thought of possible damnation.

Well-known phrases from the Old Testament often appear in the Gospels. They would have definite associations in the minds of those living at the time in which they were written. There is a Gospel phrase used to describe the result of turning away from good to seek evil, which comes from Isaiah, and it is impossible to think of a more powerful description of the agony of guilt: 'where their worm dieth not and their fire is not quenched' (Mark 9: 48). In the New Testament, warnings were given against falling into the Devil's hands, but, as in most of the New Testament teaching, what was said about him and about Hell had to be further understood and interpreted. Since it was generally believed that the essence of the Devil's work was to prevent human souls from reaching Heaven, he was later imagined to be in charge of the punishment below. In the succeeding centuries, the endless scorching flames of Hell were often conceived, by teachers and taught alike, to be a physical fire of torment.

The Jewish Cabbala, which had an important influence on the Christian Church in the Middle Ages, may have contributed to medieval ideas about Hell. The World of Matter, according to the Cabbala, is also the habitation of evil spirits. The habitations are divided into ten degrees, each one lower than the one before. The first two are absence of form and organisation, the third, the abode of darkness, but the last seven are the 'seven infernal halls', occupied by the demons who are the incarnation of all human vices. The seven Hells are subdivided into compartments corresponding to every kind of sin, and the demons torture the humans who have allowed themselves to be led astray. The Prince of this region of darkness is Samael, the evil spirit, the serpent who seduced Eve.

But of course, Hell has been, and still is, understood in numerous different ways, though almost always with the sense of retribution. John Scotus Eruigena, in the ninth century, said that Hell was a metaphor, not a locality. Hell was the permanent understanding, after death (and it was the permanence that was important), that you have got what you want; that is to say, you have achieved alienation from God in the fulfilment of your own desires, instead of what God wants for you, which is your union with Him. This seems a very terrifying form of retribution: each one gets what he wants. It implies that the 'want' must be a fixed and central one, not the continually changing 'wants' of the average person. And the complete understanding of what the fulfilment of this 'want' now means for him is the essential part of this conception of Hell.

Although John Eruigena wrote of Hell as a permanent sense of alienation, nevertheless he said that, in the end, the evil that is in every creature will be abolished, since evil is limited and all must return to God. Every creature included even the Devil. This last belief was contrary to the Church teaching of the time, but, in Eruigena's conception, when the sting of evil is finally withdrawn and all 'godding' is completed, the force that was the Devil will have no evil in it.

Origen, in the fourth century, also, contrary to orthodox teaching, had understood the final return of all created things to God to mean absolution even for the Devil. All would return to its original perfection, but, as created intelligences were given freedom of choice, the whole cycle would begin again. The Devil could start his work once more. And Origen, too, had his psychological interpretation of Hell. For him, the Devil was the epitome of chaos and lack of meaning. So Hell was purposelessness.

These conceptions of Hell do not envisage a Devil imposing punishment and torment, yet they could well include the idea of a malignant spirit, opposed to the good of mankind, enticing human beings by false suggestion, and creating influences that would prevent them finding their real good. So disbelief in the Hell of physical punishment, portrayed by medieval preachers and those of much later periods, does not necessarily mean disbelief in the presence of a malevolent and hostile intelligence. It has clearly never been necessary to believe in the existence of a goat-like, cloven-hoofed creature in order to acknowledge the possible existence of an enemy of God and Man. Moreover, the medieval representations of the Devil and of Hell in their grotesque physical forms have most certainly contributed to later reaction against belief in the existence of either.

The conception of an evil influence, whether coming from within humanity or from without, can have meaning only in relation to some kind of purpose or ideal for humankind, individually or collectively or both. If there is a corrupting and destructive power, there must be some process of development which it corrupts or destroys. If there is a force of evil suggestion, there must be some aspiration to good which it perverts. But the conception of such an enemy does not necessarily lead to the conception of Hell as a permanent place of retribution. The Enemy (whatever he may be), by creating his obstacles to development, could be preventing the human soul's growth into immortality; he may not be engaged in dragging it down to an existence of punishment, he may be engaged in seeing that it does not exist at all. It could be 'sucked into the void of non-being', as Dionysius the Areopagite had written.

Christian writers taught that, though Christ had overcome the Devil, it is necessary to obey his commands to regain the state of blessedness which the Devil had destroyed. In the story of the Fall of Man, Satan brought to the world, not only sin, but death – the loss of immortality: 'And thus it also becomes understandable that evil can be symbolised as Death, the "existing-no-more-on-the-highest-potential", and this can only be thought of as "living-no-more" ' (Mother Maria, Greek Orthodox Monastery of the Assumption, *Evil in the New Testament*). It would seem to follow that true immortality has to be earned. St Augustine said that this world was a 'world of soul making'.

Many of the great problems of existence can only be dealt with through metaphor and analogy, and the human intellect, being finite, cannot contemplate them on every level at once. Therefore, it seems that confusions will inevitably arise in trying to clarify these questions. The greatest of all confusions have probably gathered around the problem of the source of evil. Perhaps that is because the Prince of Darkness thrives on ambiguity. And perhaps that last sentence shows how easy it is to 'beg the question' and let words and metaphors pretend to solve problems.

# CHAPTER 6

# The Medieval Devil
# Rampant

By the ninth century the Devil was beginning to hold a central position in the beliefs of Christians in the West. Eastern orthodox theology paid less attention to these doctrines concerning the Evil One. The Byzantine Fathers emphasised more especially the transcendent unity of God; everything, whether it appears good or bad, coming from His hands. All proceeds from God and all returns to Him.

It seems that at all times and in all places, the more mystical and unitive the religious teaching the less place there is in it for the conception of an active spirit of evil opposing the Divine Plan. The works of the Syrian monk of the early sixth century who wrote under the name of Dionysius the Areopagite were of this unitive kind. His writings appeared in the West between about 750 and 850. They were translated by John Scotus Eruigena at the request of Charles the Bald, King of France, and had immense influence on Christian mystical thought in the West and on Eruigena himself. These Eastern teachings also influenced the writings of the Scholastic theologians of the eleventh and twelfth centuries. In their writings, as has been seen, there was less emphasis laid on the conception of evil as a hostile spirit working to destroy Man, than on the idea of evil as a privation and distortion.

In Eruigena's own time, he was unusual in giving the Devil such an unimportant part to play in the story of mankind. The concept of an arch-enemy could not easily be incorporated into his religious philosophy. Although, in accordance with the world-view prevalent in his day, he naturally assumed the existence of an evil spirit, nevertheless little attention was paid to this spirit in his writings. This was extremely uncharacteristic of Western European thought at that time.

In medieval Europe, the power of the Devil was felt to be immense. He was Lucifer, the great fallen angel who now ruled over Hell, and still aimed to overthrow God's plans and conquer Heaven. On earth, he was Satan, who never rested from his malice towards humankind. Ever-present dangers from violence and from plague gave people a sense of the world being in the grip of Satan. This sense was magnified by the teaching they received that, owing to the disobedience of their first forbears, Satan had a just claim on them. They knew that the majority of their fellow citizens were weak sinners like themselves, and few could claim that they invariably obeyed the laws of Christ, who had ransomed them only if they followed him. So few could claim to be safe from the Devil's clutches. The general understanding was of the helplessness of human beings. A tenth-century bishop of Verona was forced, in his instructions to his clergy, to stress that the Devil was *still* subject to an omnipotent God.

The teachings of some of the Church Fathers in the early centuries, such as St Jerome, had shown the Church under Christ to be the community of light in mortal combat with the community of darkness led by Satan. This doctrine, which could imply that all people outside the orthodox Christian community were of Satan's army, was later used to justify violence against Jews and heretics and those accused of being witches and sorcerers. So the ancient conception of the world as a battleground between good and evil could, and did, become the basis for persecution.

In the twelfth and thirteenth centuries, it was those accused of being heretics who were thought to be the chief servants of the Devil, for they were said to be in the Devil's army, fighting the army of Christ. In Europe, particularly in France, the heresy of the Cathars, or Albigensians, as they were also called, was the most feared, and therefore the object of the fiercest persecution. This sect undoubtedly called itself Christian, but it was violently opposed to the Catholic Church. The Cathar doctrines were largely inherited from those of the Manichees, and, like them, included belief in two Eternal Powers – the Good God and the Evil Creator of the material world. Matter was thought to be hostile to the Good, and so the Cathars also believed in the eternal antagonism between spirit and matter. The evil god, Satan, was held not only to be lord of this world, but lord over the outward man – the body that decays. They thought that, as a result of war in Heaven, rebellious angels, incited by Satan, had imprisoned heavenly spirits in terrestrial bodies to become human beings. The one aim of human beings, therefore, should be to leave their bodies and return to their heavenly home to fill the angelic places made empty by the Fall. This could be done if, at death, they were reconciled with the Good God, and had become new creatures – vehicles of the Holy Spirit.

The Cathars believed that 'The Great Church had departed from the original true teaching about Christ and his revelation, and had become immersed in materialism' (Joan O'Grady, *Heresy*). So, in their eyes, it had distorted true religion and was serving the evil god of this world. 'If a woman, supposed by her family to be an Albigensian, suddenly began to behave like a Catholic, she was said to be "possessed by the Devil" ' (Emmanuel le Roy Ladurie, *Montaillou*).

The Cathars' belief in the evil of matter led them to denounce all Catholic symbols – the Cross, the water of Baptism, even the bread and wine of the Eucharist – since, for them, pure spirit could have no connection with material objects. Because they opposed so much that was part of Church teaching, the Cathars were assumed by the Catholic Church to be in the forefront of the Devil's army and committed worshippers of Lucifer. Thus the heretics and the orthodox each believed the other to be serving the Evil One. In the twelfth century, obsession with witchcraft was still in its infancy. The fantastic descriptions, which people recounted one to another, of blasphemous rites and sinister practices connected with so-called Devil-worship were directed against heretical sects rather than against magicians and sorcerers. But the Devil was understood to be the master of both.

The sense of danger from the Devil and his hosts was a constant background to life in the Middle Ages:

> We have still to remember that other – perhaps broader shadow, that darkened Mediaeval life and thought – the shadow of 'the Devil and all his works'. This was no abstraction for the peasant, but every corner of his fields

and every corner of his home were liable to harbour
some agent of Hell, who could harm him unless it were
exorcised and overcome (H. S. Bennett, *Life on the English Manor*).

Nevertheless, in popular belief, whatever power the Devil and
his minions held, there were known ways to protect oneself
from them.

It had been Christian teaching from the earliest days, that
the Devil is powerless when we arm ourselves with faith in
Christ. Many of the Church Fathers taught that the true
invocation of Christ's name, putting ourselves in his presence,
would drive away the Evil One. As is the case with many
important and difficult ideas, these teachings and other doctrines and metaphors concerning the Devil were often taken
literally or in a wrong sense. So merely repeating the name of
Christ or making the sign of the Cross came to be understood
as putting fear into the heart of the Devil and thus escaping
from him.

There are many little superstitious and mechanical gestures
that we have inherited from this kind of belief. As the air
surrounding our earth was said to be full of the bad spirits cast
out of Heaven, the habit grew up of saying 'Bless you!' to a
person who sneezed, in order to drive away these spirits,
which he might otherwise inhale. The Devil was thought to be
constantly hovering around, waiting for an opportunity to
attack; if salt were spilled, a pinch of it was to be thrown over
one's shoulder to go into the Devil's eye, since salt is associated
with purity – preservation against corruption.

So the Devil could be outwitted. Though encouraged to
fear, the people were even taught to laugh at him. Laughter
has long been understood as a useful weapon against malice,
and so it would certainly be wrong to envisage the life of the
Middle Ages as one solely full of gloom and terror.

The medieval Mystery Plays used the Devil as one of the
chief characters in their plots. He was, of course, always the
loser at the end of the story. More correct according to Catholic theology than some of the village priests and preacher-
monks, the writers of the Mystery Plays made the Devil
clearly subservient to God, his power being strictly limited. In
the plays, the Devil was continually being tricked and duped.
In fact, he was very often treated as a comic character and

played by the local buffoon. One of these plays was based on the story in the 'Apocryphal Gospel of Nicodemus', which described Christ's rescue of the souls imprisoned in Hell. It was called *The Harrowing of Hell* and was one of the most popular of the Mystery Plays. Here the Devil is shown as an object of derision and mockery, which the audiences loved.

Though breaking one's bond was thought to be one of the most reprehensible of sins, in these plays and in many of the best-loved fables, tricking the Devil by false promises was considered perfectly allowable.

The one known to be best at tricking the Devil was the Blessed Lady, the Virgin Mary. She was the compassionate guardian of beleaguered human beings. Confidence in her never-failing power of protection from the Evil One lifted some of the heavy load of anxiety from the overburdened people. In the earlier medieval period especially, the sense of a loving protectress, always fighting on the side of humanity against their wicked enemies, helped to dispel this constant cloud of fear, and is perhaps the reason why these times seem to be such a mixture of contrasts – overwhelming terror combined with enthusiastic gaiety.

Having such pity for humankind and such power to intercede with her Son, the Virgin Mary is shown in all the ballads, stories and plays which grew up around her to be continually foiling the Devil's schemes. So there was no need to go in constant fear of the Evil One, if the Virgin Mary were there by one's side. Even if one did fall a prey to him, she would soon come to the rescue.

There are many stories on this theme in a book of medieval legends, later collected by Wynkyn de Worde in the sixteenth century. In one of these (the story has many versions), a beautiful nun, the sacristan and porteress of a convent, elopes with her lover (in some of the stories, it is the Devil himself). As she is leaving the convent doors, she passes a statue of Our Lady. Sadly, she places the keys of the convent before her, saying, 'Oh Good Lady, I have served you as devoutly as I could, and I resign my keys to thee, for I may no longer bear the temptations of my flesh.' Fifteen years later, miserable and disillusioned, she returns to her convent, where she finds that Our Lady has been taking her place as sacristan, saving her from dishonour and the Devil's clutches.

'The Special Joys of Our Lady' were the subject of many

*The Harrowing of Hell.* Engraving by L. Thiry, after
Primaticcio Barlsch.
Warburg Institute

poems, ballads and sermons. They give expression to the confident, happy side of life in the Middle Ages. The 'Joys' start with Mary's conception and end with what was the completely accepted belief of the time, her Assumption into Heaven. In the poems and ballads, the Devil and his demons howl with rage when they hear of her assumption, for they realise that human beings now have their great protectress to work for them in Heaven and to plead against the Devil on their behalf.

Belief in the power of a heavenly protectress made the position of women, in connection with the Devil, a strange and complicated one. The veneration given to the Virgin Mary, Mother of God, had been gaining in importance since the fourth century, and by the early Middle Ages she occupied a vital place in Church doctrine and in popular devotion. The importance of the feminine principle in religious belief was becoming increasingly emphasised and so entered into popular understanding and into the general outlook on life. This led in some degree to the raising of woman's status.

In literature there had existed for centuries the idea of the ideal woman. Although gentle and submissive, she was seen to be, in a sense, more powerful than man, for the chief attributes of the ideal woman were compassion and steadfastness, and these could overthrow the forces of evil. So, in trouble and disaster, the man could turn to her to save him from himself and from the powers of evil. The ideal woman is found in the Old Testament, and in many Old Testament stories; in the New Testament, it was the women who stood at the foot of the Cross; in Anglo-Saxon literature, the noble abbess was often the leader and the judge, and the dispenser of mercy; in the Age of Chivalry, the goal of each worthy knight was the approbation of his lady. The true woman also possessed true wisdom. In a twelfth-century Church play, *The Mystery of Adam*, one of the earliest written in England, the serpent was given a speech which exemplified the contemporary outlook in a joking form. The serpent said that he was tempting Eve because she was so much more intelligent than Adam. Adam was dull, hardly worth the trouble of deceiving:

Devil:   Adam I've seen, but he's too rough.
Eve:     A little hard!
Devil:   He'll soon be soft enough!

Eve:    He's very frank!
Devil:  Say very low!
        To help himself he does not care;
        The helping you shall be my share . . .
        You have much the greater sense.
        Your will is all intelligence.
        Therefore it is I turn to you.
        (*Mont St Michel and Chartres* Modern English
        rendering. Henry Adams.)

The epitome of wisdom and of the true intelligence that belongs to the ideal woman was then understood to be the Virgin Mary, and so Woman, fully realised in her, was seen to be the arch-enemy and conqueror of the Devil. In Genesis 3:15, the Lord God says to Satan, 'I will put enmity between thee and the woman, and between thy seed and her seed.' So, from the beginning, it was Woman who was the appointed antagonist of the Evil One.

This was the accepted outlook, and the outlook of the Church. But, in accordance with the writings of the Church Fathers of the early centuries, there was, at the same time, a totally contrary view of the role of women. It was they who were said to be the temptresses of men, and they who procured men's downfall. In some of these writings, it would appear as if women had no part to play in creation except as instruments of the Devil and as temptations which had to be overcome. These attitudes were the result of the dualist Manichean tendencies within Christianity. Such tendencies led to the understanding that material flesh, meaning in this context everything to do with the body, was evil. It followed from this that anything connected with the sexual relationship was part of the Devil's domain, and, with this idea in mind, women were naturally seen from the point of view of the danger which they presented. In this sense, they were the Devil's agents. This view of women in relation to the Devil had nothing to do with the later beliefs that there were people who had sold themselves to him to become witches. Women were the Devil's agents, not by any particular volition, but merely by being what they were. Women were thus in the strange position of being protectresses from the Devil and, at the same time, possible instruments for his attacks; though most often, in everyday life, both roles were taken from them, and their position was merely a hard and subservient one.

Despite these contradictory versions of the role of women in relation to the Evil one, it never seems to have been suggested in theological writings that the Devil had a feminine gender. Although there exist numerous stories about wicked female spirits and temptresses, such as Lilith, the rebellious first wife of Adam in Jewish legend, the leader of the forces of evil is always described as male. But it must be admitted that St Ignatius of Loyola, in his *Spiritual Exercises*, depicted the Devil with some of women's less salubrious features: 'Ignatius of Loyola (d. 1556) even saw typical female guile in the devil' (Marina Warner, *Alone of All Her Sex*).

Pictorial representations of the tempting of Eve have occasionally shown the serpent with a female form to emphasise the role of Woman as seductress. Michelangelo's *The Original Sin* in the Sistine Chapel, is an example. But in Jewish scriptures, in the New Testament, in the writings of the Church Fathers and in the scriptures of the other world religions, the Devil is emphatically male. In many religions, the opposite principle – the principle of growth and fruitfulness – has been personified as a goddess. But the focal point of evil, the evil principle, is almost invariably conceived in a masculine form. The Devil is always spoken of as 'he' – 'he', the Prince of Darkness. The centuries-old understanding, which seems to be fundamental to all religions, of an active male principle and a passive female principle operating through all the levels of the universe, may be part of the explanation. If there *is* a hostile force in action against humanity, this force is automatically interpreted as masculine.

There has not been a generalised picture of an ideal man in literature as there has been of an ideal woman, possibly because writing, until recent times, has been the prerogative of men, and they presumably looked for and needed this ideal. Modern women dislike being made into an ideal – 'being put on a pedestal'. But in their dislike of the conception of an ideal feminine role and ideal feminine attributes, there is a danger that some of these attributes – gentleness, compassion and steadfast acceptance – may be downgraded and diminished, so that men lose the ideal model that seems necessary for them, and women become something less than they were meant to be. In medieval eyes, this would be seen as the way the Devil was getting his revenge on women.

Throughout the Middle Ages, it was firmly believed that the

**Das xxxiij. Capitel.**

Jß sind vnd werden die zeychen sein/dabei man jn
wirt erkennen: Er wirt schwarze fleckichen haben
am leibe/vnd wirt einen heßlichen leib haben/von
braun

*The Two Monks.* From prophetic tract published Augsburg, 1549.
Warburg Institute

Devil understood the majority of human beings to be in his power, so it appeared obvious that he would concentrate his demonic forces on those who might possibly escape him. The more a person's life was centred on religion, the more powerful seemed to be the attacks by these demons, and the greater the danger of his being tempted into blasphemy and sacrilege. Those who were seriously aspiring to sanctity had, it was thought, much the most to fear, which seems to make sense in whatever way these spiritual attacks are understood. But this type of belief could, and often did, lead to hysteria.

The thirteenth century can be said to be the time when fear of the Devil was at its height. Monks and nuns of that age were often obsessed by the thought of Satan and his demons. The belief that the devilish attackers could assume physical shape meant that they were often understood to be part of, or the cause of, natural disasters and physical harms. Some monks and priests said that, in order to distract them from devout attention at Mass, which was the greatest of all weapons against the Devil, Satan and his demons would transform themselves into fleas and lice and invade their garments. They were then so tormented that they were unable to say Mass or preach to their congregations. So the Devil, in popular belief, was thought to enter into every aspect of life, and to assume any form that forwarded his schemes. The devilish host was also understood not only to cause harm and danger through external disguises, but to enter within and to represent the shameful and unacknowledged desires which arise unbidden and unexplained. This background of fear meant that, for many people, Satan was seen everywhere. And so it was not surprising that any unfortunate occurrence or unusual happening would be attributed to those who had traffic with the Prince of Darkness. Visible enemies seemed easier to combat than invisible ones.

In all parts of Europe, old folklore beliefs still persisted. Church teachings were interwoven with the old beliefs. Springs and wells, for instance, once held sacred to the worship of pagan gods and goddesses, had, in the past centuries, often been rededicated to Christian saints. Pagan festivals and old agricultural rites had been adapted and incorporated into the Christian calender. Christmas itself is an example of such a reinterpretation. December 25th had been a Mithraic festival to celebrate the winter solstice, the birthday of the unconquered sun. The venerable Bede related that, for the ancient people of the Angli, also, this date was a festival, ushering in the New Year.

The use of ancient tradition to aid in the conversion of pagans had been part of Christian practice from the early centuries. Pope Gregory the Great sent a letter, in the year 601, to the missionary saint, Augustine, telling him so to order matters that

> . . . the people will have no need to change their place of concourse; where of old they were wont to sacrifice cattle to demons, thither let them continue to resort on the day of the Saint to whom the church is dedicated, and slay their beasts, no longer as a sacrifice to demons, but for a social meal in honour of Him whom they now worship. (Bede quoted in H. S. Bennett, *Life on an English Manor*).

Nonetheless some of the old pagan belief in fearful supernatural agencies lingered on through the centuries among the peasants and the uneducated masses.

In the latter half of the fourteenth century, accusations of sorcery in the service of demons were becoming increasingly numerous. This type of fear did not only belong to popular belief, but became a part of official Church teaching, and strong measures of suppression were taken against anyone thought to be dealing in necromancy. In 1366, the Council of Chartres ordered anathema to be pronounced against sorcerers in every parish church every Sunday.

It was now held that the Devil made use of willing human beings to be his agents in furthering his evil designs. Through these agents, the sorcerers and witches, every kind of harm and disaster could be manufactured. In 1484, the Papal Bull of Innocent VIII, *Summis Desiderantes Affectibus*, declared Western Europe to be infested with demons and witches. It was affirmed that these had definite existence, and that the performance by witches of evil and supernatural operations was an irrefutable fact. After reading this Papal Bull, two Dominican Friars, Friar Henry Kramer and Friar James Sprenger, together compiled a huge, comprehensive work, describing the powers and performances of witches, their relationship with demons, and what should be the judicial proceedings against them. This work was known as the *Malleus Maleficarum* – 'The Hammer for Witches' (*maleficarum* was the term given to the evil-doing of witchcraft, particularly that of making pacts with the Devil). In the document, it was stated that the Church Fathers had agreed that there existed witches and sorcerers in Europe, so that 'To deny the existence of witches is contrary to the sense of Canon Law. People who hold that witches do not exist are to be regarded as heretics.' Innocent VIII strongly approved of this work and he appointed the two friars as Inquisitors, with special duties to investigate and stem the dangerous spread of sorcery.

It was believed that adepts in demonological rites worshipped Lucifer. These people were said to believe that Lucifer and his fallen angels would, before long, re-enter Heaven, overthrowing the Archangel Michael and his angels, who would then take their place in Hell. Stories about the evil practices of heretics, witches and sorcerers were interwoven with stories connected with these beliefs – beliefs which were naturally looked on with horror by the mass of church-going Christians. There were exceedingly few who questioned the powerful activity of the Evil One and his servants, and their continuous threat against the Christian community. The theological faculty of the University of Paris formally rejected the incredulity of such sceptical people.

The full horrors of witch-hunts in Europe, and the persecution of anyone who, on whatever pretext, was thought to be in league with the Devil did not reach their height till the fifteenth and sixteenth centuries. But belief in fantastic and terrifying accounts of the evil activities of so-called witches and sorcerers had already been growing in earlier years. Babies were said to be slaughtered and eaten as sacrifice; there were tales of monstrous animals being worshipped and horrible blasphemies being performed. With minds full of such fears, the eccentricities of an old village woman would appear to her neighbours as a sign of traffic with the Evil One, and would lead to her punishment and death. Superstition combined with fear can cause intolerable harm.

Throughout the Middle Ages, belief in the miraculous powers of the interceding Virgin was felt to curtail the power of the Devil, whatever the surrounding dangers. After the Reformation, devotion to the Virgin Mary having been largely suppressed, it was often felt that there was no one who would protect and intercede for humankind, and that the Devil had all the power; hence the ever-growing atmosphere of fear. It was this fear that led to all manner of cruelty and persecution, under the guise of fighting against the Devil. When at last, towards the end of the seventeenth century, reaction set in against these cruelties, belief in the Devil's servants, the witches and warlocks, and their magic powers began to fade, though these ideas took a considerable time to disappear completely from the general outlook of normal life. Vanishing belief in these Devil-agents led to vanishing belief in the Devil himself. A rationalistic and scientific age, such as the eighteenth century, naturally condemned the superstitions that had led to so much misery and cruelty. So it rejected the whole concept of a spiritual force of evil and therefore rejected the duty and necessity to be on constant guard against it.

It can be seen how teachings of the Church Fathers concerning the Devil, like so many Christian teachings, became distorted, so that Christians often acted in ways directly opposed to Christianity. Fighting for the Church against the Devil produced actions that could well have been instigated by him. This kind of distortion would seem to exemplify the work of the Father of Lies as it has been described from the earliest times.

The literal and, to us, childish attitudes towards the Devil that we read about in any history of the Middle Ages are often treated with a certain amount of contempt; but something may be learned even from these simplified conceptions of the Devil, if only to realise the effects that belief or non-belief in him may have. The harm that has been caused by intense fear of mankind's evil enemy is obvious enough. But this very fear could lead to awareness of the danger of temptation and the need to be constantly on guard against the sudden unexplained suggestions that drag downwards. Temptations and suggestions were believed to come from a hostile spirit working to destroy mankind. Fear of this spirit was often full of superstition, but it was not necessarily always destructive. A struggle against the unseen, but individually active, enemies of humanity gave life a meaning; and this outlook continued, in some form, for many centuries after the late Middle Ages: 'If mankind had to choose between a universe that ignored him and one that noticed him to do him harm, it might well choose the second. Our own age need not begin congratulating itself on its freedom from superstition till it defeats a more dangerous temptation to despair' (E. M. W. Tillyard, *The Elizabethan*

*World Picture*). As Origen said, Hell is purposelessness. If that is so, many people today must have a glimpse of it, for much of what we imbibe from the present-day climate of thought leads to Macbeth's view of life – that it

> *. . . is a tale*
> *told by an idiot, full of sound and fury,*
> *signifying nothing.*

Just as it is difficult, in speaking or writing about the Devil, to distinguish metaphor from statement of presumed fact, so it is difficult to separate superstition from belief. Belief itself is of many different kinds. There are beliefs held through long tradition – so long that they are rarely questioned; there are beliefs that appear rational and therefore sensible to hold; there are emotional beliefs; there are beliefs based on experience and the understanding arising from that experience; and there are beliefs held because of trust in something or somebody higher than oneself, beliefs to which one commits one's whole being. And all these can be intermingled. They can, alas, also be intermingled with superstition.

Because the Devil is described as a supernatural being, the epitome of all that is harmful, his name conjures up fear. And fear of something unknown, mysterious and possibly imaginary is the basis of superstition. Superstition has been defined as 'any belief held by someone who has not fitted it into a coherent world view' (J. B. Russell, *Lucifer, the Devil in the Middle Ages*). This definition makes it appear imperative that, in dealing with a subject such as the principle of evil, one must keep one's world-view clearly in mind. When studying religious teachings, philosophical theories, or even legends about the Evil One, it would seem vital to hold on to this idea in order to find a useful way to think.

# CHAPTER 7

# Pacts with the Devil

A very ancient belief that may be traced back to antiquity and certainly to biblical times is the conviction that human beings can gain knowledge and power through contact with supernatural, elemental forces, and through the use of laws that lie outside normal human comprehension. To achieve this contact, a complicated and difficult art had to be mastered. The practitioners of this art did not necessarily wish to use it for harmful ends; in fact, their desire could be quite the opposite, and their aim could be to reach spiritual understanding unobtainable by ordinary means. But, from earliest times, the belief that such practices existed was interwoven with the belief that certain men, in order to gain knowledge beyond that of normal human beings, would sell their souls to the Evil One. This was the worst sacrilege, and therefore fiercely condemned in the Old Testament:

> There shall not be found among you anyone . . . that useth divination, or an observer of times, or an enchanter, or a witch, or a charmer, or a consulter with familiar spirits, or a wizard, or a necromancer. For all that do these things are an abomination unto the Lord: and because of these abominations the Lord thy God doth drive them out from before thee . . . For these nations, which thou shalt possess, hearkened unto observers of times, and unto diviners: but as for thee, the Lord thy God hath not suffered thee so to do. (Deuteronomy 18:10–14)

King Solomon, since Old Testament times, had been regarded as an example of the wisest of men. His knowledge and wisdom embraced all natural sciences: 'And he spake of trees, from the cedar tree that is in Lebanon, even unto the hyssop that springeth out of the wall: he spake also of beasts, and of fowl, and of creeping things, and of fishes' (1 Kings 4:33). Subsequent Jewish legends held that he also knew the language of beasts and birds and how to communicate with unseen forces. Despite the commands given in Deuteronomy, many Jews, and later, Christians believed that, through the acquisition of wisdom such as Solomon possessed, one could master all arts and sciences. Demons could be mastered through the power of God, who had made all spirits, both good and bad. Throughout the succeeding centuries, therefore, books containing descriptions of occult and magical arts were written using the name of Solomon or claiming descent from him.

The earliest surviving example of these writings is the *Testament of Solomon*, which probably originated in Palestine in the first century. This book concerns medicine and magical arts connected with medicine. For many centuries, pseudo-Solomonic writings of this kind were being produced. But from the twelfth century onwards, books written under the name of King Solomon, but of a quite different order, began to appear in Western Europe. These were books written specifically as manuals on the art of conjuring spirits.

Innumerable pseudo-Solomonic books, dealing with the occult, were circulating in Europe in the next few centuries. They gave details of the rituals to be employed in order to perform works of magic, the words of invocation to be used and sometimes the names and powers of each particular demon who might be summoned. Some of these late medieval works were collected and translated by Reginald Scot, in 1584, in his vast book, *Discoverie of Witchcraft*. Here he gives a comprehensive list of the demons of ritual magic, who are clearly recognisable as the fallen angels, part of Satan's host. One of them is Berith,

> . . . a great and a terrible duke, and hath three names. Of some he is called Beall; of the Jewes Berith; of Nigromancers, Bolfry: he commeth forth as a red souldier, with red clothing, and upon a horsse of that colour, and a crowne on his head. He answereth trulie of things present, past and to come. He is compelled at a certeine houre, through divine vertue, by a ring of art magicke. He is also a lier, he turneth all mettals into gold, he

adorneth a man with dignities, and confirmeth them, he speaketh with a cleare and a subtill voice, and six and twentie legions are under him. (Quoted in Norman Cohn, *Europe's Inner Demons*)

From the thirteenth century, belief in the existence of magic and in the power of a magician to invoke demons for his own ends was universal – among the people and among Church leaders. Witchcraft had been accepted by the Church as a reality from the earliest times; the Mosaic Law included it as a definite crime: 'Thou shalt not suffer a witch to live' (Exodus 22:18). In the eyes of the Church, the criminality of witchcraft consisted in forming a pact with evil. The synod of Elvira (fourth century) pronounced witchcraft to be one of the canonical sins – apostasy – and to be punished by the refusal of communion, even on the deathbed. St Augustine laid down (*De Doct Chr.* II.22) that witchcraft depends on a pact with the Devil. And throughout the Middle Ages the Church looked with great severity on any form of magical art that appeared to involve the idea of a pact.

The writers in medieval times who claimed to be magicians would strongly deny that they, in any way, owed allegiance to the Devil. On the contrary, they would declare that the demons had to be controlled and mastered by the magician to do *his* bidding. These magicians claimed that they would perform no evil deed to gain the favour of the Prince of Evil. They said that the powers they sought, and claimed often to have achieved, came through the power of God, and that their success depended on the correct use of Divine words and the Divine name. From the early centuries onwards, ritual magic in both the Jewish and the Christian tradition followed the same pattern. In order to perform this magic, it was necessary for the magician to undertake a strict preparation, which included a long period of chastity, fasting and prayer. Some of the books explaining the lore of magic maintained that, if the magician were not in a state of grace or if he had a conscience that was not completely clear, then the demon could command him instead of the other way round.

Many centuries later, at the end of the nineteenth century, a French occultist and writer, Eliphas Levi (known also as the Abbé Constant, although he never actually became a priest), wrote in his book, *Dogme et Rituel de la Haute Magie*:

Magic, which the men of old denominated the Sanctum Regnum, the Holy Kingdom or Kingdom of God, Regnum Dei – exists only for kings and for priests . . . To attain the Sanctum Regnum, in other words, the knowledge and power of the Magi, there are four indispensable conditions – an intelligence illuminated by study, an intrepidity which nothing can check, a will which cannot be broken, and a prudence which nothing can corrupt and nothing intoxicate. TO KNOW, TO DARE, TO WILL, TO KEEP SILENCE, – such are the four words of the Magus . . . which can be combined after four manners and explained four times by one another. (Quoted in P. D. Ouspensky, *A New Model of the Universe*)

So, according to this nineteenth-century writer, and according to the medieval specialists on ritual magic, possession of the magical powers in which they believed could be gained only through the highest kind of spiritual endeavour.

There have been, of course, throughout the Middle Ages as well as up to and including the present day, numerous books about magic. Pseudo-occultism is rife today – spiritualism of every kind, as well as secret societies playing with witchcraft and Satanism. Until recently, this type of society was confined to a small circle. For a long while there had been so little general interest in such ideas, that it was as late as 1951 before Parliament bothered to repeal the Act which had made witchcraft a crime.

It is a strange anomaly that, although the present-day climate of opinion rejects the idea that there is a hostile evil spirit which can influence human beings to think and behave badly, yet there appear to be groups of people in the West who believe that they can get in touch with spirit forces beyond this world for their own various aims. Self-hypnosis plays a great part in these activities. The nineteenth-century French writer quoted above, lays stress on this: 'The effects of the probations, the perfumes, the mirrors, the pentacles, is an actual drunkenness of the imagination, which must act powerfully on a person otherwise nervous and impressionable.' Although he himself carried out experiments which made him feel that he had proved the positive efficacy of this type of magical ceremony, he was careful to write that 'For the rest, I regard the practice as destructive and dangerous.' Apart from the harm caused by hysterical imagination, many would agree with him that it is destructive and dangerous to dabble with forces that are not understood and which could open the way to evil. But the very sense that there is danger in such practices assumes the possible existence of evil intelligences, external to humanity. Perhaps the only conclusion to be drawn from these various opinions and beliefs is Hamlet's.

> *There are more things in heaven and earth, Horatio,*
> *Than are dreamt of in your philosophy.*

This saying, used by Hamlet to confound his friend, has since been used by everyone else unable to prove to a materialist that his five senses will not teach him everything.

The most interesting of the instructions found in the old books of occult practices was the art of imprisoning devils in black bottles. This idea arose from a legend coming from the East. It was told that King Solomon, the wise one, had discovered the secret of imprisoning devils. He enclosed them in a bottle and cast the bottle into a deep well near Babylon. But the Babylonians found it, and, thinking that it contained treasure, they broke it open and the devils escaped, returning immediately to their place of origin, where they had been caught. This legend is found in many of the oldest books on Solomonic lore and in some of the writings in the Jewish Cabbala. The art of imprisoning devils in bottles is mentioned by Gervase of Tilbury and by Gerson, writers and scholars of the thirteenth and fourteenth centuries. The importance of this aspect of magic lies in the emphasis given to the strenuous work that has to be undertaken before any devil can be imprisoned. In the oldest books it is said that only by the practice of abstinence, by strenuous self-discipline and by the use of special prayers can this be done.

What was understood in the late Middle Ages by this particular art it is difficult to discover. Certainly there were many who treated it completely literally. There were tales current everywhere of magicians who used spells and incantations to enclose demons in rings or in mirrors or in phials, and so bind them to their service. This kind of ritual magic, involving traffic with demons, was outlawed and abominated by the Church, whether the motive for the performance of magic was for good ends or for bad.

The writings of St Thomas Aquinas show that he had no doubt that demons actually come to a magician who invokes them, even if in an invisible manner. It is hard for us to understand this nowadays. Norman Cohn writes, in *Europe's Inner Demons*, 'For Aquinas, any human being who accepts help from a demon, in the hope of accomplishing something which transcends the powers of nature, has entered into a pact with that demon.' According to Aquinas, this means that a man is giving to the enemy of God worship that belongs to God alone, and is therefore committing the most heinous of sins. Such a pact had, then, the same inner meaning as the ancient conception that a man may sell his soul to the Devil to gain power for himself.

Stories and legends about a compact with the Devil had had a long history. There was a Persian belief that Eblis had made a pact with the Arabian Prince Zohar, and this type of belief was transmitted to the Jews and entered into the Book of Enoch, and, through the Book of Enoch, into the Cabbala. The Church Fathers enlarged on this conception of evil, and St Jerome quoted from Scripture to verify its existence. He used Isaiah 28:14–16, which said:

> Wherefore hear the word of the Lord, ye scornful men, that rule this people which is in Jerusalem. Because ye have said, We have made a covenant with death, and with hell are we at agreement; when the overflowing scourge shall pass through, it shall not come unto us: for we have made lies our refuge, and under falsehood have we hid ourselves.

A famous and popular legend concerning pacts with the Devil was that of the sixth-century archdeacon of Cilicia, Bishop Theophilus. This story was translated from the Greek in the ninth century and soon spread all over Europe. It appeared in England soon after 1000. The story told of a Greek priest named Theophilus, who was deprived of his post as bishop. In great distress, he made a pact with the Devil, who promised to clear him of the false charges made against him, in return for the gift of his soul. After seven years had gone by, Theophilus repented of what he had done and prayed to the Virgin Mary to save him from the Devil's power. She procured from the Devil the signed parchment which was Theophilus' contract, and gave the parchment to him. Theophilus cast it into the fire. It was considered perfectly acceptable to cheat the Devil, and so Theophilus did public penance for having trafficked with the Evil One, and died in peace. The story of Theophilus was later closely connected with the Faust-legend, the archetype of all myths depicting the selling of a man's soul to the Prince of Darkness. It is a story that has had great influence on the literature of Europe and on the imagination of the West.

It is known that Faust, or Faustus, was a historical person. He lived in Germany in the beginning of the sixteenth century, and was known to his contemporaries as a wandering charlatan who lived by his wits, proclaiming himself to be a diviner and astrologer. But there are also contemporary descriptions of him as an evil man who possessed supernatural powers through being in league with the Devil. Faust made every effort to secure widespread notoriety, and in this he was successful. By the end of the century, he had become, in the popular mind, the chief of all necromancers. Wizards who used the forces of darkness to gain hidden knowledge were now for ever associated with the name of Faust.

In the plays and stories about Faust, Mephistopheles comes to him as an emissary from Lucifer, 'chief lord and regent of perpetual night'. In Marlowe's play, Mephistopheles answers Faust's question, 'And what are you that live with Lucifer?', with these words:

> *Unhappy spirits that fell with Lucifer,*
> *Conspired against our God with Lucifer,*
> *And are for ever damned with Lucifer.*

The various versions of the *Fausti Hollenzwang* 'Faust's Harrowing of Hell' (a manual ascribed to the historic Doctor Faustus, showing how to deal with the powers of Hell) describe Mephistopheles as one of the seven great princes of Hell. He is also understood to be one of the evil demons of the seven planets. His connection with the planets is thought to have been transmitted from the ancient Akkadian religion, through the Chaldeans and Babylonians to the Jewish Cabbala and then on to astrologers and magicians of the Middle Ages.

There are several possible derivations of the name of Mephistopheles. One of these comes from the religion of Mesopotamia, in which the Intelligence of Jupiter was known as Marduk, 'Lord of Light'. The antithesis of this Heavenly Being was therefore conceived as the Lord of Darkness; and the word, 'Mephistopheles' was assumed to come from the

*The Sorcerer*. Hans Schaufelein. Augsburg 1511.

Greek – 'he who does not love light'. Another possible deriva-
tion comes from the Hebrew: 'Mephis' meaning 'destroyer' and
'Taphel' meaning 'liar'. Both derivations seem understandable;
the latter is particularly likely, as all names in the magic books
of the sixteenth century were based on Hebrew.

The acquisition of a type of knowledge which seemed to be
beyond that possessed by ordinary men had, for a long while,
given certain learned scholars the reputation of Wizard. During
the Middle Ages, there had been philosophers and writers
whose erudition made it seem, not only to the unlettered
majority, but to the educated also, that such an accumulation
of knowledge could only have been gained by supernatural –
and therefore wicked and dangerous – means. Such men were
Roger Bacon, philosopher of the thirteenth century, and, in
the tenth century, Gerbert, later to become Pope Sylvester II.
Pope Sylvester, whose scholarship and research were often in
advance of his time, was assumed, soon after his death, to
have been guilty of trafficking with the infernal powers.
Legends grew up concerning his name. He was accused of
having stolen from the Saracens a book containing 'all that is
to be known'. It was said that he had in his possession a
sculpted head, which he had had cast for him, that would
answer any question he might wish to ask. Strange pieces of
evidence such as this were produced in order to prove that he
had sold his soul to the Prince of Darkness. By these devilish
means, it was asserted, he was able to achieve his grandiose
ambitions. The legends about Pope Sylvester and the selling of
his soul for knowledge lingered on for many centuries.

It is obvious to those who read history today that scholars
such as Gerbert and Roger Bacon had little interest in
demonology or in manuals on necromancy. But that there
were magicians who literally made a bargain with the Devil
was accepted as a fact by most people, and at all levels of
society.

Since the thirteenth century, the Church had equated the
practice of magic with heresy. Every type of ritual magic was
assumed to have connection with a devil-pact. Such a pact
meant apostasy from the one true God, and so was a heresy of
the worst order. Anyone who was suspected of being a witch
or a magician would therefore be treated in the same manner
as a heretic and be brought before the Inquisition. Later, the
secular arm of the countries of Europe co-operated in the

arrest and trial of witches, in this case, relating the crime of necromancy to evil practices against the populace. There were also those who themselves believed, or were induced to believe, that they had sold their own souls to the Devil. There were old women, who through self-induced hysteria or through the pressure of their persecutors, were convinced that they had indeed made the infernal contract.

A sceptical attitude was rare and the growth of scepticism very gradual. Towards the end of the seventeenth century, a French writer, Jean Uvier, expounded a rationalist view, and it was demanded he should be sent to the stake for his temerity. In England, only a very few of the most sophisticated would have appreciated Shakespeare's teasing of the bombastic Owen Glendower:

Glendower:  I can call spirits from the vasty deep.
Hotspur:    Why, so can I, or so can any man;
            But will they come when you do call for them?
Glendower:  Why, I can teach thee, cousin, to command the devil.
Hotspur:    And I can teach thee, coz, to shame the devil
            By telling truth: tell truth and shame the devil.

Today, there is no one, except perhaps those who play with Satanic cults, who believes that it is literally possible, in return for some benefit, to sign a contract with an entity called 'the Devil'. But the belief that a man might be willing to sell his soul is a powerful one, and has entered our literature and our language. We speak of someone selling his soul for political power or material gain. But what is meant by this? 'What is a man profited, if he shall gain the whole world and lose his own soul?' (Mark 8:36). We certainly have the sense that it is possible to value some unworthy object so highly that we are willing to prostitute the highest part of ourselves in order to gain it. St Thomas More is reputed to have asked Richard Rich why he made this sale merely for Wales!

If we associate the Devil with the expression, 'selling one's soul', we are now more likely to mean, not so much that we have made a bargain with an evil power, but that the evil power has induced us to give up our integrity in return for wealth, security or position. The actual bargain is usually made with some person or persons who are able to give us those things which we crave. The evil influence which encourages us to do this, whether or not we term it 'the Devil', belongs to the sphere especially associated with the 'Father of Lies'. A good is sought that is not a true good and has to be paid for dearly. In fact, the same deception is played here as was played on Adam and Eve.

The Gospel story of Christ's Temptation in the Wilderness shows this theme of false values on the highest possible level:

> Again the devil taketh him up into an exceeding high mountain and showeth him all the kingdoms of the world, and the glory of them; and saith unto him, 'All these things will I give thee, if thou wilt fall down and worship me.' Then saith Jesus unto him, 'Get thee behind me, Satan; for it is written, "Thou shalt worship the Lord thy God, and him only shalt thou serve." ' (Matthew 4:8-10).

Belief in supernatural powers that bring good or harm to men, and belief that these powers can be placated by man or even harnessed to serve him, have existed from the most ancient times. But strange to say, though it has been believed that demons can be conjured up by magic ritual, and that these demons will give to the magician superhuman knowledge and power, a belief that good spirits can be invoked to bring such magical gifts has never existed in the same way. The rare instances of attempts at angelic magic have looked to quite other results. Belief in the Devil and his host of demons seems to have been in a different context from belief in Archangels and the hierarchy of angels. But if one is trying to understand what is meant by the term 'Devil', and what has, through the centuries, been understood about him, perhaps one should try to understand also what the opposite term, 'angel' signifies, and this is considered in the next chapter.

# CHAPTER 8

# The Angelic Host

It seems that, in all traditions, supernatural beings who act as messengers of the Supreme Being have been part of religious belief. They are the intermediaries between earth and Heaven. In the scriptures of many religions, a human being's experience of relationship with God is expressed through a description of his encounter with an angel.

It was orthodox Christian doctrine, and finally formulated in the thirteenth-century Lateran Council, that God 'by His almighty power, simultaneously, at the beginning of time, fashioned out of nothing the spiritual and corporeal creation; that is – the Angels and this world; and afterwards the human race, commingled, as it were, of spirit and body'. Angels were said to be pure spirits, endowed with intellect and will. St John Chrysostom had written in the fourth century that 'God not only produced created things but also watches over and cherishes them, whether you term the powers "angels" or "archangels" or "superior powers", or all those things which do or do not come under our senses.'

In Ezekiel's vision of the destruction of Jerusalem, there are seven great angels. The number seven is thought to be connected with the seven planetary divinities of the Babylonian religion, the Jews having been in contact with this religion during their exile. A relationship between planets and angels appears in the cosmologies of many religious systems. Some Gnostic schools, in the centuries following the birth of Christianity, gave to the seven archangels, as shadow counterparts, the seven planetary demons.

From very early days, the name 'angel' signified the office which was performed, rather than the actual being. This office was primarily the role of messenger: 'They cannot always be spoken of as "angels", for they are such only when things are declared by them' (St Gregory the Great).

Dionysius the Areopagite, whose doctrine on the hierarchical system of the universe and of Creation had such immense influence on the religious thinking that came after him, based his theology of angels on what he read in the Old Testament and the Apocrypha, and in the epistles of St Paul. He was also influenced by Neoplatonic thought, which held that each step in the hierarchical descent from the All-Perfect was a step away from living reality, a diminution of spirituality and a diminution of being.

In his *Celestial Hierarchies*, Dionysius compares God to a ray of light proceeding into manifestation. As the light descends, it is graded into an order, a hierarchy, which leads down from the angels to mankind, and, through the natural order, to formless matter.

Dionysius describes the angels as 'theophanies' – symbols of God, giving form to that which is formless. Thus 'a divine light is shed upon the seers . . . and they are initiated into some participation of divine things'. This initiation 'is passed down, as it were, in a chain from the higher to the lower ranks, till mankind receives it from the Angels. Thus one might say that, for man, every theophany (appearance of God) is in fact an appearance of an Angel' (Peter Lamborn Wilson, *Angels*).

There were said to be nine choirs of angels because nine names for heavenly powers are mentioned in Holy Scripture; and these are also the nine orders described by Dionysius: they are Angels, Archangels, Virtues, Powers, Principalities, Dominions, Thrones, Cherubim and Seraphim.

The Seraphim were said to belong to those of the highest order and were the guardians of Yahweh's sanctuary. They are mentioned by name only once in the Bible, in Isaiah 6:1,2 'I saw also the Lord sitting upon a throne . . . Above it stood the Seraphim; each one had six wings; with twain he covered his face and with twain he covered his feet; and with twain he did fly.' Tradition held that the Seraphim inflamed mortals with divine love.

The word 'Cherubim' in Hebrew means possessors of wisdom and of the fullness of knowledge. Moses was told to carve two Cherubim on the mercy seat of the Ark. In Ezekiel's vision, the Cherubim had each four faces – the face of a cherub, the face of a man, the face of a lion and the face of an eagle, and each had four wings and 'they sparkled like the colour of burnished brass'. The Cherubim were the bearers of Yahweh's throne or chariot, and, in Genesis, after the expulsion of Adam and Eve, they were placed at the eastern entrance of the Garden of Eden with 'a flaming sword, which turned every way, to keep the way of the tree of life'.

The third of the highest order of angels were the Ophanim, the Thrones, or Wheels. They surrounded the Most High. Ezekiel describes them as fiery wheels with a ring of eyes, and as the mounts of the Cherubim. The Dominions, the Virtues, the Powers and Principalities were titles given to the other great angels from names of powers mentioned in the scriptures, in Daniel, in the Apocrypha, and in the Epistles of St Paul.

In the Book of Enoch, which, of all the Apocryphal books exerted the greatest influence on subsequent generations, the seven Archangels are given their hidden names, and their powers and functions. Michael, whose name in Hebrew means 'who is like God', is here said to be the greatest of them all and to hold the secret of the mighty 'word' by which God made Heaven and Earth. To him was given the task of overthrowing the rebel angels, and therefore, St Michael is always portrayed as commander of the angelic hosts of Heaven. He is described in the Apocryphal book as being set over the best part of mankind and over Chaos.

The names of some of the Archangels given in the Book of Enoch are little known, and it is difficult to understand what is meant by the functions allotted to them. There is Uriel, who rules the world and Tartarus; Raguel, who takes vengeance on the world of the luminaries; Saraquel, who is set over the spirits; and Remiel, whom God set over 'those who rise'.

The other two Archangels have more familiar names and functions. Raphael means, in Hebrew, 'God heals'. In the Book of Enoch, he is called 'the angel of the spirits of men' and is the angel of healing. Gabriel means 'the strength of God' and was said in the Book of Enoch to be ruler of Paradise, the serpents and the Cherubim. He shares in the work of intercession, and so has been shown, above all, as the greatest messenger of God. In the New Testament, it is Gabriel who is sent to announce the birth of Christ, and of John the Baptist, the forerunner of Christ.

Yahweh, in Ezekiel's vision, was surrounded by his serving

angels, the Holy Ones. Throughout the Old Testament, angels of different functions are shown as the intermediaries between God and Man. There are the angels of punishment, the angels of death who visit the dying, the protective angels and the angels who carry prayers to the Most High.

In the Jewish scriptures, it can be seen how the greater the stress laid on the absolute transcendency of Yahweh, the greater is the importance given to angel intermediaries – intermediaries between the Infinite and the finite. When a Divine command or instruction was given to a prophet or leader of the people, it was revealed by an angel of the Lord.

The religion of Islam, which has great veneration for the writings of the Old and New Testament, also maintains belief in angelic powers. The Archangel Gabriel is said to have appeared to Muhammad in order to reveal to him the sacred book of the Koran; and in that book it is written that the angel Gabriel declared the coming of Christ to the Virgin Mary. Again the transcendency of God necessitates an intermediary. Gabriel told Muhammad that 'God is veiled by seventy thousand veils of light and darkness, and, if these were swept aside, even I would be thoroughly consumed.'

The New Testament has many mentions of 'angels'. For example, Christ himself speaks of them. In his teaching on the consummation of the world, he says, 'And then shall he send his angels, and shall gather together his elect from the four winds, from the uttermost part of the earth to the uttermost part of heaven.' The Gospel tells how, after the Temptation in the Wilderness, angels were sent to minister to Christ. And, in Mark 8:38, Christ says 'Whosoever, therefore, shall be ashamed of me and of my words . . . of him also shall the Son of man be ashamed, when he cometh in the glory of his Father with the holy angels.'

The Book of Revelation is full of references to angels, for it speaks of the last times – the Last Judgement and the consummation of the world – and here uses the imagery of the Old Testament and the Prophets. The work of the angels is on the vast scale of creation and of the end of creation.

The Old Testament speaks of the angels of nations, and, though sometimes connected with the tribal gods of the nations surrounding the Israelites, the angels of nations became understood as the spirit and ethos of a people. Origen, writing in the third century, says that the angels set over the nations are responsible for the fact that each religion possesses Truth: 'The secret and occult philosophy of the Egyptians, the astrology of the Chaldeans, the Hindu claims pertaining to the science of the Most High God . . . each of these princes has a separate science and a special doctrine to teach' (quoted in Peter Lamborn Wilson, *Angels*). Clement of Alexandria, to whose lectures Origen had listened as a boy, had also expounded these ideas. He said: 'It is the unique Word, which has given out to each nation, through the angel set over it, the form of wisdom proper to it. Wisdom is one in principle but multi-form in presentation' (quoted in Daniélou and Marrou, *The Christian Centuries – The First Six Hundred years*). The conception of a spirit inspiring and guarding each nation was never a definite part of Christian dogma. But the conception of a spirit inspiring and guarding each individual person was understood in a less metaphorical way, and entered into orthodox Church teaching.

St Basil, Bishop of Caesarea in the fourth century, wrote: 'It is the teaching of Moses that every believer has an angel to guide him as a teacher and shepherd'; and St Jerome also said 'Great is the dignity of the human soul, since each one of them has, from the very outset of his life, an angel deputed to safeguard him.' So it seems that, from the earliest centuries, the Church had expounded the doctrine that each soul has a guardian angel. The verse in Matthew 18 was understood to confirm this: 'Take heed that you despise not one of these little ones; for I say unto you, that in Heaven their angels do always behold the face of my father which is in Heaven.' (Matthew 18:10)

It is clear that the conception of 'angels', in the various religious traditions of the world, centres around their function as intermediaries between a transcendent, infinite Being and finite, limited human beings. They have been thought of, metaphorically and literally, as appearances of God in a visual form – a form that human minds are thus able to experience. They have been conceived as forces of good, maintaining and directing, in different ways and in different spheres, the development of the created universe. In their relation to the individual, when they are regarded as Guardian Angels, they might have been interpreted as the highest part of the spirit within each person, perhaps only rarely encountered as a living experience. In the tradition of Islam, it has been held by some that Man is capable of ascending and becoming, himself, an angel. And there is a Christian legend that the thrones in Heaven made vacant by the fallen angels are reserved for the elect among humanity. So, in the same manner that Dionysius the Areopagite had described the descending hierarchy of the universe, there could be described an ascending ladder, reaching to the Archangels. Beyond them, the visions of the prophets become too hard for us to interpret.

The Church, from the beginning, emphasised the importance of angels, though the actual worship of them was discouraged. St Paul had warned against this and against assuming that one could easily understand what was meant by the terms 'angel' and 'archangel'. He said: 'Let no man beguile you of your reward in a voluntary humility and worshipping of angels, intruding into those things which he hath not seen, vainly puffed up by his fleshly mind' (Colossians 2:18). But, at the Council of Nicaea in 325, belief in the existence of angels was stated to be part of Christian dogma.

Though the Eastern Church has continued to have a particular veneration for doctrines concerning the archangels, and icons portraying their functions and the principles which they contain are revered in the Orthodox Church as objects of great holiness, there has been decreasing significance given to the concept of 'angel' in the West. This may be partly due to the way artists have depicted them, particularly since the Renaissance. In the first descriptions in the Old Testament, angels were described as terrifying, awe-inspiring beings, differing totally from anything found in human experience. The association of wings with the idea of rising, and being lifted above ordinary humanity, made it understandable that the figures of angels, in the same way as the Seraphim in Ezekiel's vision, should be portrayed as winged beings. In some of the scriptural stories, the angels sent from Heaven to give commands or messages, appeared as shining, resplendent men, or as men, who were only recognised to have been angels after they had disappeared. But pictures of angels, in later centuries, have tended to be sentimentalised, so that any sense of awe and transcendence vanishes. The most vivid example of this enfeeblement of the concept of 'angel' is seen in the treatment of the Cherubim. The awe-inspiring angelic powers with four faces and four wings, who barred the way back to Eden with a flaming sword, have become chubby little baby boys with curly hair and rosy cheeks. A cherub, in today's terminology, is far removed from the great being, guarding the throne of the Most High.

Lucifer, in both the Christian and the Islamic traditions, was once the most beautiful of all the angels, with the special charge to watch over mankind. His fall, caused by the egoism of his self-will, transformed him into the opposite of what he once was. The name of Lucifer, the great fallen angel, the light-bearer, became synonymous with Satan, the adversary, whose watch over men had now become a watch for the weaknesses in them, where suggestion could lead to their destruction. Tradition, too, based mainly on the Book of Enoch, held that Satan's host of devils had also once been part of the angelic host of Heaven. As time went on, the great fallen angels became, in the medieval imagination, a swarm of wicked little demons, engaged in every kind of mischief, small and great. Nevertheless, the conception of angelic beings, intermediaries between God and man, was essential to the theological concept of a Spirit of Evil, the constant opponent of mankind. For it was from a corrupted angel-intermediary that the Prince of Evil came.

Belief in the existence of spirits, good and bad, and in the account of how they became so, is not necessarily the same as the understanding of why these terms were used as explanations, and of what they were used to explain. In the Middle Ages, people of all levels of society, and whatever their degree of education, accepted these explanations in a more or less literal way. They used these descriptions to interpret their picture of the universe, instead of using descriptions given by scientists as we do. Both methods of description and interpretation have their limitations.

Belief in the power of good angels to protect and inspire was never so strong, nor so universal, as belief in the power of the fallen ones to inflict harm. Until the 'Age of Reason', the idea that there were initiates, who had mastered the secret arts and thus possessed the magic powers by which they could summon spirits to their aid, was a general belief. It was also generally understood that the spirits that were summoned were demons or elemental forces, and even those magicians who maintained that their magic was of a high and noble order would insist that they were controlling the demons and forcing them into their service. It was only during the period of the late medieval and post-medieval witch dementia that it was believed that magicians became the servants of the evil spirits, or, more often, of the Prince of the evil spirits. Prior to this it was the magician who was the master. But the invocation of spirits, even if it were claimed that they were being used for good ends, never pretended to be the invocation of angelic powers. It seems to have been understood from the earliest times that these angelic powers were on a different scale, and that it was not possible to imagine their relationship with human beings in the same way as the demons' relationship was imagined.

There were some rare cases when it could be said that there was a study of 'angelic magic'. For instance, it was claimed, in the time of the Renaissance, that from an ancient Egyptian book, the *Corpus Hermeticum*, some writings had been rediscovered which gave instructions on how to call down angels and planetary spirits. Pico della Mirandola, an Italian philosopher and writer who produced theosophical and mystical studies on various aspects of Christian thought, is said to have worked on these discoveries with his friends among the Florentine scholars. The interest in these theories was never widespread, and little seems to have become known about them. It is likely that these early writings would be more akin to teachings on the ancient Mystery Religions and to the rites and symbols used in them, than to manuals on the magic arts of invoking the power of demons.

Though, in the early centuries, it was accepted that human beings had the possibility of using demons for their own ends, and that, by the performance of certain acts and by the reciting of certain words, protection could be gained from these evil spirits, there has never been a general belief that good spirits could be reached and influenced by rites and ceremonies in at all the same way. Perhaps it was believed that immeasurably greater power was needed to reach *them*, or even that the very pursuit of power was part of the Devil's domain.

In subsequent and more sceptical times, the belief in an evil being with his subordinate minions, hovering around us and constantly ready to attack, became, in general opinion, outmoded and discredited. But in these later centuries, there have been, and still are, small groups of people strongly attracted towards the idea of a demonic power in the world. In fact, scepticism and superstition have curiously been found to go together.

# CHAPTER 9

# Rationalism, Scepticism and Superstition

In the sixteenth century, the forces of evil were still explained in terms of a personal Devil. In spite of the break with traditional ways of thinking and the growth of secular learning which characterised the Renaissance period, fear of demonic powers continued to dominate popular imagination. The theocratic view of the universe with its basic assumption that religious traditions and customs were the centre of life was coming to an end. As a result of the Reformation, there was no longer a unified Christendom nor the assumption of a unity of Christian belief. The picture of the world seemed to have become less clear-cut, and the sense of stability, which had been part of the religious outlook, was seriously weakened. Fear of supernatural enemies remained, but without the hope of rescue by any miraculous powers of the Church or intercession from a Heavenly protectress. These hopes had till then made the fear of the Enemy easier to bear. The now unalleviated fear led to an increased suspicion of any unusual happening, or of any untoward occurrence that might be a possible indication of witchcraft.

Religious reformers attacked many of the contemporary beliefs and customs which, they said, had grown up as accretions on the original Christian doctrine. But they still accepted the medieval view of Christianity, which held that Satan possessed the present world and that mankind could not be delivered from this state of bondage except through Christ.

Calvin and his followers insisted on complete literal

*Witchcraft.* From
Philosophia Imaginum.
Claudé Francois
Menestrier, 1695.

dependence on the Bible, and therefore on the literal interpretation of every reference to 'witch' or 'devil' to be found
there. They were unrelenting in their investigation into suspected Satanic practices and in their persecution of suspected
witches. The Calvinists were largely responsible for augment-
ing the prevalent fears of demonic magic, and so for the plague
of witch-hunts that disfigured Europe in the sixteenth and
seventeenth centuries.

Belief in ever-present danger from the Devil and from the
practitioners of his Black Art had existed for centuries. But
one of the reasons for the actual formation of so-called Satanic
covens may have been the insistence of the witch-hunters,
both in the late Middle Ages and in the sixteenth century, that
the existence of practising witches and warlocks was an established fact. If possession of devilish magical powers were
accepted by the authorities as a proven reality, then the
achievement of these powers was obviously possible and
could be to one's advantage. Groups of people, mainly
women, formed themselves into covens for this purpose.

The covens of witches and warlocks were said to perform
the Black Mass, which they had made into a blasphemous
antithesis of the Christian Mass. They were said to pay homage
to the one who called himself the Devil – Satan's representative
– and to receive new converts who had come to renounce their
Christian baptism in order to join the Devil's community.
Heathen fertility rites, often of a very unpleasant nature, were
part of their ceremonies and were said to culminate in frenzied
sexual orgies. How accurate these tales are is uncertain, and
there was, without doubt, an immense amount of fanciful
exaggeration inspired by fear. But during this period many
people of both high and low degree were known to have formed
associations whose purpose was to practise various forms of
necromancy. Many people would go secretly to the village
witch for her potions and charms. They would go to her for
cures from every kind of sickness, to achieve success in love,
or to seek revenge on an enemy. It was the general opinion
that both black and white forms of magic were being practised
everywhere.

Nevertheless witchcraft was a punishable offence according
to the law of most European countries, and it was not only the
humble village folk who were liable to be suspected. For
instance, in 1593, in Scotland, Francis, fifth Earl of Bothwell

(nephew of the fourth Earl, the husband of Mary, Queen of Scots) was tried for the offence of witchcraft. He was accused of attempting to procure the death of James VI, King of Scotland (later James I of England) by magic arts, and of using the craft of witches to conjure his destruction. Bothwell was acquitted, but many local citizens had confessed themselves to be witches and warlocks and had testified against him.

The other great figure of the Reformation, Martin Luther, though not himself associated in the same way as Calvin with the terrors of witch-hunts, firmly believed in the existence of a personal Devil, the leader of a host of subordinate devils. He believed that this Devil even caused plagues and infirmities. The fires of Hell and the shades of Purgatory were vividly present in Luther's mind from childhood on. In his eyes, sinful man deserved these punishments. Luther's mental and spiritual struggle to understand how he, as an erring mortal, could ever escape from Hell and damnation finally brought him to the realisation that pardon could be obtained by trusting in the promises of God. Once he had acquired this sense of peace and deliverance from his mental torments, he committed himself to the belief that trust would lead to pardon and salvation. What had appeared to him to be a hopeless struggle with ascetic practices and imposed penances, he now understood to be unnecessary.

Nevertheless, the Devil was still very real to Luther. There is the well-known story of how, in his cell, intensely concentrating on his writings, he was interrupted by the appearance of the Devil, in the guise of a huge black dog. Determined to be free from the Devil's mastery, Luther, with all his force, hurled his heavy inkpot at the beast, who instantly disappeared. This story and other descriptions of manifestation by Satan were believed as literal truth by the majority of people for a long time to come.

By the end of the seventeenth century, revulsion against the horror of the witch-hunts and the cruel persecution of so-called sorcerers and heretics had caused a strong reaction against all ideas and beliefs concerning the Devil. There was a weariness with fanatical dogmas and self-righteous bigotry. The sight of Protestants and Catholics alternately putting each other to death produced the desire to say: 'A plague on both your houses.' These reactions were confirmed and encouraged by the new and developing studies of nature and philosophy.

New discoveries were being made, and people were becoming confident that the world was subject to intelligible laws and was not a mystery under the inscrutable designs of God. By continuing to discover these laws, it was thought that Man would be able to control his environment and so, by his own efforts, grow to perfection. No longer did he consider himself a fallen creature, in danger from Satan and dependent on the powers of Heaven for his well-being, but looked to his own rational powers and to the tools of science to build an ever-improving future. It was the period of 'the Enlightenment'. In the eighteenth century, later to be called 'the Age of Reason', there was no longer any room for the Devil as an explanation for evils soon to be eliminated.

The religion most favoured by the intellectuals and upper classes was a type of Deism. This was supposed to be a reasonable, universal, natural religion. Scripture and tradition were to be subordinated to the human powers of reason. To create a reasonable ethic was said to be the end-product of religion. John Toland, who lived between 1670 and 1722, wrote, in his *Christianity Not Mysterious*, that nothing is above the comprehension of the logical mind. The French Revolution enshrined the worship of reason. In France, churches were designated 'temples of reason', and statues of the Goddess of Reason appeared in Notre Dame and numerous village churches. It was now said that it was central to the rational understanding of religion that there were no mysteries.

Merging with this type of rationalist religion was what would seem at first sight to be its opposite. This was Romanticism. It was a movement aiming to base religion on feeling, rather than on intellectualisation and dogma. But though it appeared that, in this movement, reason was to be kept in the background, romanticists were close to the rationalists, in that both types of religious outlook emphasised the perfectibility of Man. His perfection was the inevitable outcome of his onward progress. Jean Jaques Rousseau may be called the father of this type of romantic thinking. He was also, as it later appeared, the father of those intellectuals who did not study humankind as it is, but based their philosophies on what they imagined it ought to be.

Another reaction against the fanaticism of previous centuries was a movement known as Pietism. It was also a challenge to the eighteenth-century worship of reason. Like

Romanticism, Pietism maintained that the heart of religion had been lost in a maze of intellectualising. But its exponents were very differnt from the romantics. They taught a Bible-centred moralism and, above all, a keen sense of human guilt and the need for personal conversion. Religion had to be expressed outwardly in good works and active participation in community devotions.

Methodism has been described as the greatest expression of Pietism in the eighteenth century, and Methodism is for ever connected with the name of John Wesley. The Wesleyan movement was a great force that rekindled the waning sense of religious fervour in England. This was especially so among the merchant and working classes. Evangelical pietism was a powerful reaction to formalised religion and to the limitations of rationalism. But Wesley himself still lived under much of the thought-atmosphere of more ancient times. He believed in the Devil's power to manifest himself in any shape he wished, and this belief was naturally connected with his fear of the dangers of witchcraft. He maintained that, in so far as God permits, evil angels are 'governors of the world'. Satan and his demons war against mankind and arouse evil passions and infuse evil thoughts. In considering beliefs in an existing, personified Devil, it is often difficult to determine whether or where to attach the label of 'superstition'; and on this account, it is not a simple matter to arrive at a correct assessment of Wesley's conception of Man's Enemy.

John Wesley was living in an age when discoveries were being made that altered the way in which it was natural to view the universe. But, for Wesley the world was still a battle-field. He held to his firm belief in the direct sovereignty of God and the final overthrow of the Enemy. The rules which he drew up for his Methodist societies were for all those who had a 'desire to flee from the wrath to come'. The Enemy, who would entice them into this wrath, had for him a very real existence.

During the century of 'Enlightenment' and 'Reason' and for several decades after it, there were groups of people, mainly comprising rich young men in Society and members of exclusive literary circles, who believed neither in the God of the Evangelists nor in the God of the Deists, and whose confidence in the new discoveries that were being made in the natural sciences made it impossible for them to believe in the God feared and worshipped in the Middle Ages. They thought themselves superior to the ignorant masses who still believed that the world had actually been made by an omnipotent Divine Being; though they believed, or said they believed, in a malevolent spiritual being, who presumably had made himself.

The devil-beliefs of the young blades of Society probably should not be taken very seriously. The groups and clubs which they formed were more likely set up in order to shock and outrage respectable citizens than as an attempt to summon or serve the Devil.

In England, in about 1719, a typical club of this sort was founded by the young Duke of Wharton. He called it the Hell-Fire Club, and its aim was said to be the promotion of sacrilege. The Devil was its president. For this sinister president, a chair was kept vacant during the club's meetings. There have been many lurid stories about the Hell-Fire Club and its Black Masses, and several other similar societies are known to have sprung up in imitation of it. But there is little accurate information as to what actually went on at any of these meetings. All that is certain is that Wharton's club was finally banned by royal proclamation on account of its 'horrid impieties'.

The end of the nineteenth century and the twentieth century itself, the age that, above all, is the age of science and technology, has seen a proliferation of groups with an interest in occult and demonic 'sciences' of a much more serious nature. At the turn of the century, members of such groups were likely to be of an aesthetic turn of mind, who fancied their intellectual and artistic achievements and looked down on people whom they considered to be imprisoned in outworn religious beliefs. There were groups of this kind in France, Germany and England. Three occultist groups in France – one headed by the novelist, J. K. Huysmans, the others by a Spanish marquis and an unfrocked priest respectively – regarded their rivals with such bitter hatred that they endeavoured to cast demonic spells upon each other. They each accused the others of using their magic arts with the aim of encompassing the deaths of their rivals, and, during this quarrel, one of the protagonists did die. The members of the secret fraternities firmly believed that his death was the result of sorcery.

In England, too, there were societies being formed which had the aim of discovering ways to get in touch with the world of spirits and demons. The most famous of these was the Order of the Golden Dawn. This society concentrated on the translating and decoding of what they held to be important magical textbooks, such as the 'Key of Solomon' and the mystical parts of the Cabbala. While in its heyday, the Order of the Golden Dawn had numerous lodges, and numbered among its members writers such as W. B. Yeats and Algernon Blackwood. But, as seems to be inevitable in this type of society, fierce quarrels broke out between its leaders. Aleister Crowley, whose name later became famous in connection with black magic, joined the Order, and immediately began to use every means possible to take over the leadership of it. When at last the existing leader died, many members of the Order were convinced that Crowley had killed him by the use of magical arts. During their period of dispute, both contestants were said to have harnessed to their service vampires and demons in order to destroy each other. Crowley lived until 1947, continuing to practise unpleasant 'satanic' rituals and delighting in a reputation for wickedness. He gave himself the title of 'The Great Beast'.

It seems incredible that educated men, living in an age renowned for its scientific discoveries based on reasonable hypotheses, could have believed in the fantastic and often ludicrous happenings and ideas accepted as truth by these self-styled adepts. But, as G. K. Chesterton once said, a man, discarding his religious traditions, does not believe in nothing; he believes in anything. So these groups regarded, as part of an old-fashioned and outmoded shibboleth, the notion that there exists a power of Goodness, responsible for creating the world and for laying down a design for it. But they were ready to admit the possibility of an existing spirit of evil, whose forces could be contacted and used for the manufacture of super-human powers. The definition of superstition as a 'belief that is not fitted into a coherent world-view' very accurately describes this type of credulity.

Interest in magic has continued to spread in recent years. There are now many societies calling themselves covens of witches in England and America, and many books written on how to enter the witch-sisterhood. Some of these societies are based on the attempted resurrection of what are held to be ancient pre-Christian religions. Their members would not consider themselves to be aiming at contact with infernal powers. But there may be a few who would term themselves Satanists, and who, presumably, give central place in their activities to the Prince of Darkness.

There are certainly people today who believe that fellow-ships owing allegiance to Satan exist, and that Satan can keep even unwilling participants in his power. A case was recently brought to court (D. Mainwaring Knight, 1986) in which several wealthy members of a parish church and the vicar of the parish himself were induced to part with large sums of money for the purpose of buying back from a Satanist society certain artefacts of Satanic regalia. This was alleged to be necessary in order to ensure, for a repentant member of this Satanic sect, freedom from the Devil's power and from the clutches of the Satanists. Whether or not such a sect really existed, and, if it did, whether or not it did all it was claimed to do was not shown. But clearly, those who brought the accusa-tions of fraud had originally held a strong enough conviction of the existence of Satanism for them to give thousands of pounds to attack it. The fraud appeared blatant from the start, but belief in the possibility of traffic with supernatural forces of evil seems to have been more powerful than common sense.

The cult of witchcraft which was originally presumed to denigrate and overturn everything Christian arose, it has been said – referring both to the past and to the present – through antagonism to the strict demands of Christian teaching. In the past, it could be described as a revolt against the regulations of the Church, and, in the present, as a desire for liberation from the restrictions held to be part of a conventional Christian life. In both cases, the rites and practices associated with the cult of witchcraft are assumed to express opposition to accepted values, and freedom to act on this opposition.

It has been affirmed by some religious philosophers, for example St Anselm and St Thomas Aquinas, that no one desires evil in itself. People desire what they think to be good for themselves, however harmful and destructive it may in fact be. Those who were held to have worshipped Lucifer in the past were said to do everything that was contrary to Chris-tian commandments and accepted human behaviour, and to use Christian symbols and sacraments for every kind of blas-phemous purpose in order to reverse the established order. This was not so much because they desired evil as because they hoped to gain unlimited power for themselves through the forces opposed to Divine laws. Students of black magic and Satanism, in modern times, also appear to be aiming at the rejection of the Good figure, as conceived through the ages, in favour of what has been conceived as the Evil one. This would seem to entail a liberation from all restraint and from all that is held by common consent to constitute the normal conditions of life. Again, the practitioners of these 'satanic arts' would say that this was not for the purpose of achieving evil for its own sake, but in order to gain the possession of supernatural power.

The subject of Satanism and Devil-worship is a complicated one because it has, throughout history, been confused with the study of magic, and the two are not entirely the same. The art of magic, as understood in the ancient books, such as the Cabbala, was always connected with the discovery of hidden laws beyond the plane of ordinary knowledge – laws of nature and of the spirit. It is difficult to dismiss as make-believe all stories about strange and seemingly magical happenings, both in the past and in the present, and especially those tales from isolated country districts, where the people are insulated from modern urban life and are still in possession of ancient inherited customs. We do not know enough.

There is in existence today a people, numbering about sixty thousand, who are known as Devil-worshippers – the Yezidis of Kurdistan, Armenia and the Caucasus. They were originally Muslim, but their practised religion has its roots in old Iranian and Assyrian beliefs, with traces of the teachings of the Manichees. They worship Satan, as the great fallen Archangel, now pardoned. Satan, once Lucifer, the creative agent of God, became the author of evil. The Yezidis believe that, now pardoned, he has been given the government of the world and the management of the transmigration of souls. It is known that the expounder of their faith was a Sheikh Adi, who lived in the thirteenth century and that they have a sacred book, called the Al Yalveh. The Devil, for the Yezidis, is represented by the peacock, and his name must not be spoken out loud. But it does not seem, from the little that is known about them, that these Devil-worshippers aim to possess unlimited demonic power, as the modern 'Satanists' are said to do. So it seems that here, yet again, is a different type of 'Devil-worship'.

Another problem, connected with all kinds of occultism, is

that of disentangling the fake from the real. In relation to questions of religion, psychology and mysticism, how to achieve this disentangling is, in modern times, probably the greatest of all difficulties. Pseudo-religious teachers, pseudo-spiritual cults, and pseudo-occult societies abound.

There seems to be a miasma of delusion, intentional or unintentional, surrounding all that pertains to the mystical. The very word 'mystical' has acquired meanings which exemplify the muddle we are in. Originally it meant 'having a certain spiritual character by virtue of a connexion, or union, with God, transcending human comprehension' (*O.E.D.*). It still has this meaning in relation to certain types of religious writings and experiences. When, however, in the eighteenth century, reliance on the power of logical reason to answer all religious questions became part of the accepted outlook, the word 'mystical' came to imply a type of belief 'associated with self-delusion and dreamy confusion of thought' (*O.E.D.*). It is often used today in this derogatory sense. Again, 'mystical' can be a synonym for the mysterious, the unknown, the supernatural. So, merely using the word 'mystical' to describe what are understood to be occult studies and practices can give rise to very different interpretations and expectations concerning them.

Imagination plays a very great part in gatherings that attempt to invoke spirits and make contact with demonic powers. Intense use of the imagination can cause a type of hallucinatory vision, or even a manifestation. This use of the imagination has, sometimes, in the past, been taught as a part of religious instruction and as a way of meditation. P. D. Ouspensky writes in *A New Model of the Universe* that 'A very amusing parody of these methods is to be found in Eliphas Levi's book, *Dogme et Rituel de la Haute Magie*, where he describes an evocation of the Devil. Unfortunately very few readers of Eliphas Levi understand that this is a parody.' Imagination can be a powerful and dangerous instrument, especially when it is unacknowledged and out of control. Those who are under the sway of imagination and do not try to use their intelligence in a sensible way, are liable to be governed by superstition. As Edmund Burke said, 'Superstition is the religion of feeble minds.'

The Romantic school was largely responsible for the now fairly common view that the word 'good', when applied to a person, describes him as rather uninteresting and lacking all fire and audacity; while, on the contrary, a bad or wicked person is seen as strangely exciting, so that it is especially fascinating to hear about him. This kind of meaning attached to 'goodness' and 'badness' is a fairly modern one. In the past, and in many Eastern countries until very recent times, the generality of people regarded 'goodness' and 'holiness' with awe and veneration. When the aim for freedom of expression and thought became dominant among writers and thinkers in Europe, the restrictions of the old orthodoxy became the barrier that had to be overleaped. Conventional thought and behaviour then became interlocked with the term 'goodness', and were felt to imply a drabness of being and a bar to creativity. But the view which we have inherited from the Romantics leads into a kind of superficial thinking that becomes ever more superficial through the automatic categorising of people into stereotypes.

It is true to say that, through all periods of history, everything to do with evil and with spirits of evil has exerted a fascination over human minds. Stories about devils have been, on the whole, more popular than stories about angels, and accounts of evil doings will sell more newspapers than accounts of good deeds. It is much easier to portray Hell in painting and in literature than it is to portray Heaven. Pictures of Heaven tend to infuse a sense of intense boredom. The idea of standing around in Heaven, wearing white robes and singing endless hymns, inspires very few people with a longing to go there. True goodness and real glimpses of Heaven are rarely met with, but most people have met, in themselves and in others, touches of evil, and many people, at some time in their lives, have had a glimpse of what Hell might be like.

The strange tendency in human beings to be drawn to stories of evil, whether through fear or merely through curiosity, gives the Devil, however he is understood, a very great advantage. Through this tendency, people can be brought under influences of a definitely harmful kind, their minds and emotions having been opened to them. But it has been said that the Devil who attacks us, however wily he may be within his sphere, is very stupid beyond it, because he has no footing there. He overplays his hand. So people who, through being caught by evil suggestion, have had a glimpse of Hell, may very well do everything in their power to gain help, in order not to go there. Great sinners have become the greatest saints.

The word 'saint' has also been periodically imbued with a totally false sense, that of weak and watery priggishness. But it is probable that it is only through the existence of authentic saints, rare as they may be, that the forces of evil, or, if it exists, the Evil Intelligence itself, can be defeated. If it is true, as it might seem, that destructive forces, acting through human minds, can disrupt civilisations, then the converse may be possible. Creative forces, acting in the same way, might stem a flood of evil, if there should exist enough channels of the right calibre through which they could flow.

# CHAPTER 10

# The Subjective and Objective Devil in the Modern World

The writers and philosophers of the nineteenth and early twentieth centuries, like those of the eighteenth, were, in general, full of confidence that Man, as a rational being, would make continuous progress towards self-betterment, and evil tendencies would automatically be checked.

The tenor of philosophical writing was becoming less sceptical towards religious ideas. As entrenched religious bigotry and fanaticism grew weaker, so there appeared to be less need to attack them. The ancient problem of the origin of evil was still discussed, but the general climate of opinion was one which called for rational explanations, and, in this instance, a rational explanation of that which had, through the ages, been called 'the Devil'.

Students of the Bible, particularly those of a fundamentalist persuasion, aimed to retain the conception of the Evil One in their doctrines, but without its medieval accretions. The idea of a personalised Devil was considered pagan and superstitious, and not in accordance with the religious teaching of the day. Protestant teaching had, for a long time, equated demons with particular vices and used them in a strictly metaphorical sense.

The scientific discoveries of the new age continued to encourage the belief in an ordered universe, governed by natural laws. These laws were seen to be subject to human comprehension. Interference in this order by supernatural powers from the Beyond was now held to be alien to a correct view of the universe. This meant that the evils and misfortunes which beset mankind could no longer be ascribed to demonic forces.

Philosophers and clerics, when writing about evil and the forces of evil, now aimed at providing explanations which would be acceptable to reasonable and well-balanced minds.

Kant, the greatest philosopher of the eighteenth century, had opened the way to this view. His understanding of 'the Devil' was grounded in the rational. For him, 'the Devil' was the personification of the evil that is in Man. He took the concept to mean, in fact, all that can be called hatred of God, since he understood the word to express the principle of evil and this principle to be a reversal of the moral order. Evil, as he conceived it, had come into the world through an unexplained propensity in human nature. Kant's philosophy confined all that we call knowledge to the realm of space and time, that is: to what is experienced through the categories of the mind which organise our sense-data – that which he termed the constituents of pure reason. And therefore what this evil is and how it entered humankind cannot be known, since it is beyond the categories of space and time, and therefore, beyond pure reason.

Kant believed that practical reason demanded a moral law. Reason demanded the postulates of 'freedom, immortality and God', since otherwise life would make no sense. Just as knowledge of natural phenomena, according to Kant's philosophy, was dependent on the constituents of the human mind, so religious knowledge, also, was subjective, because dependent on these postulates of human reason. Relativism and subjectivity were thus introduced into the philosophies of the coming centuries.

Philosophical methods and manner of approach to religious debate now differed considerably from those of earlier times. From now on, the sources of religious conceptions and beliefs were to be investigated and questioned. Previously, traditional legends and stories that had been handed down through the ages were accepted, and then studied by writers and theologians with a view to interpreting the value of their meaning. The theologians also aimed to discover how these stories were connected with the accepted body of religious doctrine. It is only in relatively modern times that it is considered important to question how certain beliefs have arisen.

Though philosophical discussion about the origin of evil and how best to define it has continued throughout the centuries, the exact meaning of the concept of the Evil One had never been discussed in those terms. That is to say, the origin of the concept had not been the subject of debate.

In the nineteenth and early twentieth centuries, it was not fashionable to consider the problem of evil in terms of an evil power called 'the Devil'. Scientific explanations had been found for many of the biological and psychological phenomena that had previously bewildered mankind. Satan, it seemed, could be safely ignored. If he were mentioned in religious philosophy, it would be more in the sense of how his concept had arisen than of how *he* had arisen. Discussion about him had become increasingly abstract. It could be said that the Scholastics were obsessed with theoretical definitions in their arguments about the focus of evil, and so their discussions were also metaphysical and abstract. But, in accordance with the thinking of their age, they inevitably accepted as the basis of their discussion the existence of a supernatural danger, a threat to themselves and to all humanity. Ideas about religion and philosophy have, since Kant, tended to stress subjective experience and understanding at the expense of objective doctrine. And so a sense of danger has never entered this type of writing. Anything that could be termed evil was shown to be explicable in terms of human mental and physiological processes.

There was also in this period a tendency – one which has to a certain extent remained with us – to believe that only scientific knowledge, knowledge about facts that can be weighed, measured and mathematically justified, is true. All else seemed to belong to metaphysics, which had become an unpopular discipline and viewed with mistrust.

Western Europe had now entered the secular age. The validity and value of religion, *per se*, was being questioned more universally than they had ever been before. Charles Darwin's *Origin of Species*, published in 1859, was having a growing influence on theological writings and on the current attitude towards religious ideas. Church leaders of all denominations were at first fiercely hostile to Darwin's theories, fearing that the Bible, as a source of truth, was being challenged and that the special spiritual status given to human beings was being denied. But gradually, the works of theologians and biblical scholars began to show that this was not necessarily the case, and attempts continued to be made towards the reconciliation of science and religion.

This reconciliation then became, perhaps unfortunately, connected with the current optimistic belief in humanity's inevitable progress. The rationalists and the romantics of the eighteenth century had emphasised the power of Man's reason and his capacity for perfection, if allowed to develop freely. These ideas were now combined with the popular understanding of the Theory of Evolution. It was assumed that everything and everyone could evolve: 'Through economic betterment, social improvement, and more education, primitivism and sin would be "evolutionized" away' (C. L. Manschreck, *A History of Christianity in the World*). The doctrine of Original Sin was rarely mentioned. And the ancient conception of weak, sinful Man, in constant danger from the wiles of the Devil was certainly no longer the accepted background of popular religious belief.

Of course this optimistic view of the human condition was not held by all writers and religious leaders, and in many quarters there was opposition to it. Nevertheless, it occupied an important place in the general attitude and outlook of the time. But, as the twentieth century proceeded, the scene changed dramatically.

During the first part of the century, the discoveries made in the physical sciences had engendered a popular conception of the universe and its contents as a huge machine, coming into being by chance and continuing to grow by chance. In the era of optimism, the assumption of a lack of conscious purpose in this machine did not present any terrors, since belief in a general upward evolution still formed the background of Western thought. But the horrors experienced in two World Wars and in the many types of totalitarian régime that then emerged, and continued to emerge, have clearly revealed what, after millions of years of 'human evolution', human beings are capable of doing to other human beings. It is probably true to say that it is now impossible for the old type of optimistic belief, based on an assurance of inevitable, universal progress towards perfection, to continue. A mechanical universe no longer seems a pleasant place in which to live, since the human part of it no longer appears to hold a guarantee of ultimate success. For many people, meaninglessness has become the chief misery of our age, and one from which they would seek any means to escape:

> *A dreary sort of Universe, inanimate and blind,*
> *Where Mind doesn't matter, and Matter doesn't mind.*
> (E.de Stein, 'From an E.C. Chair')

But, at the same time, there is a sense, which had not existed in the recent previous decades, of an evil, endangering the world and all humanity. People of the present generation have a strong feeling, as had those in the Middle Ages, that there are vast forces of violence and destruction existing all around them. There is now the added fear of total, universal destruction, through the mismanagement of nuclear power. The baser instincts of human nature do not seem to be in the process of reformation through increased education, as had been generally predicted, nor through improved economic conditions, as had also been forecast. They do not seem to be reformed through changes in systems of government, nor through social revolutions. Fear of violence, treachery and dishonesty from other human beings seems to dominate the subconscious of the people of all nations; hence the danger of war and the terror of crime.

All that has been said might make the present period appear to be one of unalleviated darkness, which is of course absurd. It is easy to find innumerable things which are especially beneficial in this age. Even though, as is bound to be the case, popular understanding of the structure of the universe is based on the scientific thought of a previous generation, many of today's physicists are discovering that it is no longer possible to make a hard and fast distinction between what has been termed 'matter' and what has been termed 'spirit'. An 'inanimate and blind' universe does not now seem to be the most fruitful hypothesis. So the discoveries of science may be leading us out of a blind alley; more people are searching, in possibly a more urgent and serious way than ever before, to find answers to their questions – answers which could have permanent value. Nevertheless, in discussing the focus of evil and what it may mean and has meant in the past, it is necessary to concentrate on all that seems to be wrong *now* – on all that could be interpreted as the consequences of an evil force, active in our world, however that force is understood.

The sense of overpowering evil that often seems to prevail in the thought and literature of the modern world – the sense that there is evil on such a scale that it is greater than ordinary human wickedness – may be partly due to certain conditions peculiar to this age: the speed of communication, which enables each part of the world to be immediately aware of what is happening in all other parts, the vast increase in populations, the technical expertise of commercialism on a huge scale, and the ever-increasing velocity of change – all these contribute to the sense of a new magnitude of evil. But however it is understood, human delight in destruction for its own sake, witnessed in vandalism and violence; sadistic cruelty seen in the actions of governments and individuals; the ever-increasing greed for money (described in an old Jewish proverb as 'the Devil's excrement'); the ruining of other people through the sale of drugs and through sexual degradation; and the vastly increased potential of nuclear power, without any increase in human wisdom to use it properly – all appear as examples of evil so great that they bring back the sense of demonic forces at work in our world.

Evil can only be made manifest through the thoughts and actions of individual human beings. But today, as in times past, many people again feel that there are influences surrounding them that are more powerful than they.

The two most dangerous influences that now pervade the whole world seem to be the glorification of hatred, and the insidious power of suggestion. The two have always been intertwined, since it is suggestion that causes people to feel that their hatred of each other is somehow virtuous. Espousing what seems to be a noble cause is often understood to give the right to hate all people who are antagonistic to that cause, or who simply do not actively support it. Even those whose aim is to promote world peace are often full of animosity towards those who think they can promote it in a different way. The desire to help the underprivileged and downtrodden is transformed into the concept of class-warfare – the very word 'warfare' assuming the necessity for a righteous hatred.

It was the same in times past. Fear of the dangers of black magic caused normally decent people to persecute and torture those whom they suspected of being in league with the Devil, with the clear conscience that they were doing God's work. All these perversions of thought and feeling seem closely relevant to the concept of a Father of Lies. But, nevertheless, though there are few today who hold the optimistic world-view held by the previous generation, it is also a minority who have a positive belief in an active spirit of evil from whom they must protect themselves. Because of this, though there could be a general feeling that there are evil forces at work in the world, there is no longer a belief in the necessity to be on guard, in order not to come within their orbit.

In the ancient stories depicting the Arch-Enemy of humankind, he is often described as dropping insidious suggestions into the ears of those whom he is aiming to tempt. It had always been held that it is by suggestion that the Evil Spirit perverts the mind of men, the classic example being the temptation in the Garden of Eden.

In whatever way 'the Devil' is conceived, it is certain that the human mind has always been liable to suggestion, and humankind being prone to error, obedience to suggestion will, more often than not, lead to harm of some sort. It is of course harder work to use one's own intelligence than to follow the suggestions of another.

Another reason why it is felt that a spirit of evil, however understood, has such power today is because, owing again to modern technological inventions, suggestion can be more universal and more insidious than it has ever been before. Advertising, newspapers, radio and television all can and do impose their suggestions endlessly on human minds. Lies, consciously or unconsciously, can be spread very quickly, and educated and uneducated alike can be influenced in their thoughts and opinions without being actively aware of it. Greed has been a basic human vice throughout recorded time, but today, with all the instruments that are available to serve it, it can have a field-day. Advertisements can continuously suggest new wants and a sense of deprivation if they are not satisfied. Providers of entertainment in all forms can ceaselessly suggest that the public want only the crudest and poorest type of amusement, and that almost anything is acceptable provided it makes money. All these suggestions come, of course, through human agency, but there remains the fundamental lie at the back of them – that those through whom these suggestions come are producers of good, if not always for the recipients, at least for themselves. The ancient deceit of false promises seems to be at work; the trick, originally ascribed to Satan, of presenting evil under the guise of good.

Though thoughts and actions can come only through individual human beings, there still remains the problem of how this universal deception arises. The influence of the lie seems to be so powerful, that it might appear to be on a larger scale than anything belonging to the human mind.

Belief in a demonic power is certainly alien to modern ways of thinking, and preachers of the last century were often keen to discourage it, as they feared people's habitual tendency to blame an exterior force for their own misdoings. Religious writers were, and still are, inclined to describe Satan as the personification of the evil that is in the world. In this view, evil comes from us, and so Satan can be described as the evil that is within us. There seems good sense in this conception, particularly as it counter-balances the general desire to slough off our own guilt. But, in accordance with many twentieth-century views on religion, the world-outlook is here made completely subjective. The danger of destructive influences, under which we may find ourselves unless we are on the watch, may be, in this view, disregarded. The ancient objective conception of 'the Devil', however superstitious it may now seem to be, had its use. It was considered important to be careful under what kind of influence to place oneself, and no one felt certain from exactly where destructive influences could come.

The main obstacle to discovering a helpful way to think about the idea of 'the Devil' is the tendency, closely connected with the emphasis on subjectivity, to believe in that in which it is comfortable to believe. It is possible that the cosmos, as it actually exists, may not be a very comfortable place for humanity. Human beings automatically think that everything is created for *them*. They desire and claim to have free will, but do not wish to take into account the accumulated mountain of human misdeeds that have piled up throughout the millennia, and have created most of the horrors about which they complain. One has often heard people say, 'I could not believe in a God who allowed such and such a thing to happen, ' as if only what one likes and approves of can have fundamental existence in the universe. These two desires – to blame one's misdeeds on something other than oneself, and to commit oneself only to beliefs that are comforting and comfortable – make it difficult to face the amount of evil that there is in the world, or to investigate where it comes from in order to be able to resist it. There is always this tendency among human beings to cling to an inner sense of comfort and security, to what Gurdjieff, in *All and Everything*, refers to as 'their inner "Evil God", called "Self-Calming" '.

In the Middle Ages, teachings about the Devil, developed by the Christian Church from the doctrines of the Church Fathers, were by no means comfortable or comforting. 'Self-calming' was only made possible by the habit of blaming all personal wrongdoing on demons or on their leader. In the teaching of many Christian churches today, there is no absolute requirement to profess a positive belief in the existence of Satan. On the whole, there is a tendency to ignore him. He is certainly seldom mentioned in sermons, or in books of spiritual maxims. In these books when the word 'Devil' is introduced, it is more often in a metaphorical sense, personalising our weaknesses and our inclinations towards harmful emotions and actions. But the present-day Roman Catholic, Anglican and Orthodox Churches include strong statements about the Evil One in their doctrine and liturgy. Many of these are based on conciliar pronouncements concerning the concept of demonic power, which have been given through the centuries. Though he may no longer hold a central place in popular belief, the name of Satan is certainly not discarded in Church doctrine, and it is necessary to find out how he is there understood.

# CHAPTER 11

# The Devil in Church Rites

There are definite formulations concerning the Devil to be found in the Roman Catholic catechisms – books of instruction in Catholic doctrine in the form of question and answer. These have been used over a long period. The most important of these catechisms was drawn up after the Council of Trent (1545–63) for the use of parish priests, 'to foster the knowledge of Christian doctrine according to the decrees of the Fathers of Trent'. There had been many earlier catechisms and there were some later ones, but often these were written for the particular needs of various regions; the Trent catechism was definitive and universal.

In 1932, a catechism for adults, with a catechism for the instruction of children, was drawn up by Cardinal Gaspari, based mainly on the Trent catechism, but incorporating anything that seemed useful from the others. In recent times, there have been several new manuals, the most well-known being the 'Dutch Catechism', termed 'A New Catechism of the Catholic Faith for Adults'. This last is in the form of a summary of Catholic belief, covering a vast area, and even including unsolved questions and problems. It abandons the old question-and-answer format, which many think can lead to a narrow and legalistic approach to religious doctrine. But it may be true that, as the compilers of St Peter's Catechism (a modern catechism of Catholic Doctrine for adults and older children, compiled in the 1970s) have written, 'Priests need firm formulas, clear statements and exact formulations' in order to give their teaching. From such beginnings, it is said, those seeking instruction can start to discover and to understand the meaning of their religion. However this may be, the

Detail of *The Doom*. York Minster.
Warburg Institute

question-and-answer type catechisms, in speaking of the Devil, make clear and definite statements.

In Cardinal Gaspari's catechism of 1932 and in the catechisms for children that were based on it, the story of the rebel angels who became 'devils' under their chief, Lucifer, or Satan, is presented straightforwardly as fact. To the question, 'What can the devils do against man?' a straightforward answer is again given. By God's permission, they can harm him in external things, 'and even to his person, by taking possession of his body, and by tempting him to sin; but they cannot prejudice his eternal salvation without his free consent.' The teachings in Cardinal Gaspari's catechism are derived from the 'Testimonies, referred to . . . from the Ecumenical Councils, the Roman Pontiffs, the Fathers of the Church and the Roman Congregation', and this last answer concerning the Devil comes from the statement of St Irenaeus, included in the Testimonies: 'All the Devil – the apostate angel – can do is to seduce and lead men's minds and so make them transgress God's commands . . . he blinds the hearts of them who would serve God . . . so, in time, they come to forget the true God and to worship the Devil as God' (*Adversus Haereses*).

In the Roman Catechism of the Council of Trent (translated and annotated by John McHugh O.P. and Charles Callan O.P.), on which the later catechisms are based, it is clearly stated that 'to our inward conflicts are added external assaults of the demons, who also insinuate themselves, by stratagems, into our souls'. This statement is founded on St Paul's letter to the Ephesians, with his strange warning against 'the rulers of the darkness of this world' who are not of 'flesh and blood'. The catechism affirms that, under this evil governance are those who, 'blinded by defilement, are satisfied to have for their leader, the Devil, the Prince of Darkness'. The wickedness is said to be 'in high places' because the chief aim of the Prince of Darkness is to deprive us of our heavenly inheritance.

It is stated in this Catechism that, 'if we put on the armour of faith', the Devil cannot hurt us, but, nevertheless, he wages perpetual war and continues unceasingly to tempt and worry us. In this Trent Catechism and in those following it, the ontological existence of the Devil and his legions is categorically affirmed, this affirmation being based on words used in the New Testament and on the writings of the Church Fathers.

There is a question in the St Peter's Catechism which asks: 'Are we bound to believe that devils really exist?' And the answer is: 'We are bound to believe that devils really exist because this is the clear teaching of Holy Scripture, affirmed by the Catholic Church.' So, despite the recent tendency to ignore questions about 'the Devil' in religious teaching and philosophy, there has been no denying his existence in official Catholic doctrine. The Trent Catechism was extremely firm on the subject. It writes: 'Many imagine that the whole matter is fictitious, since they think that they are not attacked themselves. This means that they are in the power of the Devil and have no Christian virtue. Therefore the Devil has no need to tempt them, as their souls are already the Devil's abode.'

It is the teaching of the Christian Churches that there are evil powers in the Spirit world. These powers, created good, have become evil by their own free choice. Therefore, in one sense, they have brought about a miscarriage of God's plan by their disobedience, even though, through the Divine power, all can be used for good. Since according to Christian doctrine, there is no separate principle of evil as in the doctrines of the Manichees, in Christianity, all evil is apostasy from good.

The Council of Trent stated (session VI, chapter 1): 'Whereas all men had lost their innocence in the prevarication of Adam . . . they were so far the servants of sin and under the power of the Devil and death.' It is taught that when Adam fell, he rejected the supernatural, so that, at birth, human beings are subject to the natural kingdom only. Because of the superior power of the angelic over the human nature, Satan has his dominion over men. Since he had the original nature of an angel, he can dominate those creatures who are inferior to angels. This doctrine is based on the writings of Dionysius the Areopagite, who described a hierarchy of angels, where the higher spiritual entity has power only over the lower in the scale of being. According to the teaching of the Council of Trent, when Christ's merits are applied to the individual, that human being is raised again to the supernatural order, and is then free from the power of Satan. He will still have to endure the temptations of the demons, part of the Devil's hosts, but these, like their master are within God's governance, and belong to what is called 'the permissive tolerance of God' (George D. Smith (ed.), *The Teaching of the Catholic Church*).

It is clear that, in this Roman Catholic teaching, the Devil is much more than a symbol of the evil that is in Man, or of the collective evil that comes from Man. He is not regarded as a person in the way that we think of ourselves as persons, but is said to have a personality, which is the summing up of all that we understand to be contrary to good. That there exists a disembodied intelligence, hostile to Man, is stated to be part of the Christian Revelation, and to have been given in the Old and New Testaments. In these scriptures, when speaking of the power of evil, the personal pronoun is always used. According to Catholic doctrine, belief in the Scriptures and in the traditions growing out of them requires a belief in the Devil's existence. But there is a further question that can be put: could we know of this hostile intelligence without the words of Scripture, or, rather, would we assume its existence without them?

St Thomas Aquinas wrote that the Devil's actions were only external; he can tempt to sin, but cannot cause sin. If he did not exist, humanity would still be subject to the temptations of the body, to internal passions and to fatal weaknesses. It might appear, then, that, according to some of the arguments put forward by Aquinas, reason and logic do not demand a belief in the Devil; it is acceptance of the Scriptures of the Church that demands it. But, nevertheless, there may be other powerful considerations persuading people to believe in an independently existing force of evil – a spirit-force surrounding our world, and ever ready to attack us. If there is such a force, it certainly seems appropriate to use the word 'Devil' for it.

It can be seen from the study of history and from research into the beliefs of other races, that the conception of the Devil as a being hostile to humanity and capable of inflicting evil upon it is widespread and almost universal, and has been since recorded time. But there is a stronger reason for accepting this conception than a general similarity of belief throughout time and space.

The scale of evil perpetrated in the world sometimes seems, to our perception, greater than the collective wickedness of humanity. The terrible cruelty that human beings inflict upon each other seems to be caused by something outside nature and the natural order of creation. We hear of men and women in past times flocking to watch the burning of heretics and the public execution of criminals, for purposes of entertainment;

today, we hear of parents starving and torturing their own children. On reading of such horrors, the involuntary exclamation escapes one – 'What *is* wrong with human beings?' Something terrible seems to be at work.

The experiences of the twentieth century have once more reinforced the sense of an exterior evil influence acting upon us. As Pope John Paul II has said,

> The evil which exists in the world, which encompasses and threatens man, nations and the whole of humanity, seems to be greater than ever, much greater than the evil for which each of us feels personally responsible. It is as though it grows within us according to its own inner dynamism and goes far beyond human intentions, as though it indeed came from us, but was not ours – according to the expression of the Apostle John.

This description of the force of evil is akin to that given by Clement of Alexandria, when he said that the Devil exists both inside the human mind and outside it. We do not know what that evil influence is – it manifests through human beings, through their thoughts and actions – but is it something more than them, something far more dangerous than a metaphor for our own inclinations to evil? When we talk about 'the Devil', are we personifying humanity's evil inclinations, or is there an external intelligence that suggests these horrors to us, so that we put them into action?

It can be said that answers to these questions are given in the Roman Catholic catechisms. That the Devil exists, how he operates and how he originated are clearly stated. But accepting these statements is not identical with 'believing' in him, and certainly not with understanding what is meant by the terms used. In the first place, it is necessary to discover the meaning of the story describing his origin. The events related clearly do not belong to human experiential knowledge, so that, if the story is to be included in a religious cosmic scheme, the original underlying purpose of the myth must be sought. Secondly, it is possible to 'believe' in given formulations concerning the Devil in the same way as one 'believes', for instance, in scientific formulas explaining the construction of the atom. In both cases there is trust in the superior knowledge of the formulators. Those who accept what is formulated in the catechisms trust in the scriptural interpretations given by the Church Fathers and in the ensuing Church teaching.

But real belief, in a religious sense, involves much more than taking statements on trust. In this instance, belief in the Devil and his minions has to be related to one's own 'world-view', and above all, to the meaning one gives to one's own experience. Nevertheless, the statements about the word 'Devil', as used in these manuals of Catholic doctrine, may be useful in the way question-and-answer catechisms are sometimes thought to be useful. They give clear expositions of doctrine; people who read them must then find their own way.

Today, many Catholic as well as non-Catholic thinkers are inclined to understand the word 'Devil' in a figurative sense and to regard 'the Devil' simply as the personification of all that is evil: 'Among Christians of our day there are very few who *believe* really and effectively in the Devil, and for whom this article of faith is an active element in their religious life'. (H. I. Marrou, *Etudes Carmelitaines*, 'Satan'). Most would accept the existence of the Devil only if it can be interpreted symbolically and identified with sin and with the downward trends of our human nature; and most of those who think like this would react against the idea of an independent hostile intelligence. But it has been said that 'the custom adopted by Christians, since the last century, of "demythologising Satan" often, therefore, takes on the nature of a flight from the serious exactions of the Christian situation' (Louis Monden, SJ, *Signs and Wonders*). The 'Christian situation' has been considered, from the beginning, to entail a battle against the forces of destruction – those forces previously described as the legions of the Prince of Darkness.

The words used in some parts of the Roman Catholic liturgy give clear expression to a belief in demonic existence. The spirit of evil is addressed directly as a person. This is shown especially in the rite of Baptism. The evil which threatens Man is commanded to go away.

When an adult comes as a catechumen seeking baptism, the priest breathes upon him, and orders the evil spirit to make way for the Holy Spirit. In this rite, the priest is acting as an exorcist. He is exorcising the demon of evil that is within. During the Baptism, the Devil is several times sharply ordered to depart.

In the 1969 Roman rite for Infant Baptism, the exorcism begins in the form of a hymn:

*Almighty and ever-living God,*
*You sent your only Son into the world*
*To cast out the power of Satan, spirit of evil –*
*To rescue Man from the power of darkness,*
*And bring him into the splendour of your kingdom of light.*

In all rites for the baptising of infants, the parents and god-parents, on behalf of the child, make a formal renunciation of Satan. They promise to reject 'the world, the flesh and the Devil'. The 'Flesh' has been defined as our own evil tendencies and passions; the 'World', as the false principles by which we love the goods of this world better than God; the 'Devil' is therefore treated as something separate from both of these.

In the 1969 Roman Catholic rite, the questions are asked: 'Do you reject Satan?' 'And all his works?' 'And all his empty promises?' – or, as an alternative form: 'Do you reject sin, so as to live in the freedom of God's children?' 'Do you reject the glamour of evil, and refuse to be mastered by sin?' Do you reject Satan, father of sins and Prince of Darkness?' To all these questions, the parents and godparents answer, 'I do'.

In the liturgy of the Easter Vigil, the time considered from the earliest days to be the most appropriate for baptism, the members of the congregation renew their baptismal vows. They are again asked whether they renounce Satan and all his works and wiles. And again they answer with the promise, 'I do'.

In the Russian Orthodox liturgy, also, the exorcising and expulsion of Satan is explicit and direct.

At the beginning of the Orthodox baptismal ceremony, which in former days was part of the introduction of a catechumen into the Christian community, the priest recites three long prayers of exorcism, in which the Devil is ordered to depart: 'Wherefore I charge you, most crafty, impure, vile, loathsome and evil spirit . . . Depart!'

The adult to be baptised or the sponsor of the child, if it is an infant baptism, turns his back to the altar and is asked three times to reject Satan and to spit upon him. Only then can he turn to face the altar and three times accept Christ.

The formulations of Christian doctrine and the wording of the Catholic and Orthodox liturgy thus clearly affirm the metaphysical existence of a spiritual being known as 'the Devil'. But does this necessarily lead to the belief that there is a host of lesser evil intelligences under his command, continually tor-menting and tempting human beings? The story of the Rebel

*Devils*. From the 'Livre de la Vigne nostre Seigneur' (M.S. Douce 134, f.99r). French Work of the fifteenth century.
The Bodleian Library

Angels who followed their leader, Lucifer, and whose Fall transformed their angelic nature into a demonic one, seems to imply this. According to tradition, the rebel angels, like their leader, lost their heavenly stature and dwindled to the level of Man's evil tormentors. It was certainly understood in this way throughout the Middle Ages.

Belief in these lesser devils is reinforced by the words used in the New Testament to describe the way Christ cured the sick, and the way he spoke about his cures. Evil spirits, known as 'devils' or 'demons', are mentioned in Judaeo-Christian writings from early ages onwards. If there is an intelligent force of evil operating against mankind, it is possible to conceive of it as affecting human beings through influences of greater and smaller magnitude. In the same way, it could be said that a human being can experience the power of God through greater or lesser spiritual forces or influences. The analogy is not exact, since, except in completely dualistic religions, such as Manicheism and later Zoroastrianism, evil has not been conceived as one unified and eternal being. It may be better to say that the force of evil, or the evil intelligence, which has been termed 'the Devil', could be a shifting and composite force, coming now in one shape, now in another, experienced now on a huge scale, now on a small personal one. This could mean that the powers of evil may operate differently according to the level where they are active.

Evil is told to depart from a catechumen, just as a demon was told to depart from a possessed man in the New Testament. Every priest, therefore, is, in a sense an exorcist, and in the Early Church the office of Exorcist was one of the four minor orders. But the churches also recognise a need for a different type of exorcism. This is termed Solemn Exorcism. Solemn Exorcism can be performed only by priests authorised and specially deputed to this office, and it is used only in cases of what is termed 'preternatural possession'. These cases are now said to be extremely rare, but they are definitely held to exist. There is debate within the medical profession as to whether there are such instances of devil-possession and as to whether and how they can be differentiated from psychoses and neuroses of various kinds. But the fact that cases of this sort are seriously questioned and studied shows that 'possession' in the biblical sense has to be investigated. The problem of 'possession' is a puzzling one. One single completely proven case would make it difficult, if not impossible, to reject the idea of an existing evil being. Even one case, where any solution other than 'devil-possession' is hard to find, places a large question-mark against purely symbolic interpretations of the Evil One. The phenomenon of 'devil-possession', as described now and in the past, is one closely connected with the powers and the disputed existence of the Prince of Darkness himself, and so, however problematical, cannot be brushed aside.

# CHAPTER 12

# Devil Possession

In the centuries before what is termed the 'Age of Enlightenment', it was considered normal and natural to believe that the atmosphere surrounding our world was inhabited by spirits, both good and bad. In these earlier centuries, contemporary imagination was accustomed to a world-view which showed a scene of angels and demons, ready to assist or to attack humankind. Now, 'Enlightenment's' confidence in a completely rationalistic and materialist interpretation of all phenomena is on the wane. Though the majority of Westerners no longer picture a world of good angels and evil spirits, many who in former times would have lived in fear of these inhabitants of our atmosphere, now speak instead of the occult forces, which surround humanity and which can use or be used *by* it. Clairvoyance, thought-transference, telekinesis and out-of-the-body experiences are all phenomena which have been attested, though not satisfactorily explained. Again, the atmosphere seems to be alive with strange influences, often termed the occult, and again the borderline between gullible superstition and sensible belief is hard to distinguish.

In Old Testament times and earlier, illness had an animistic interpretation – all sickness was understood to be brought about through the intervention of a spirit. This meant that insanity of every kind was attributed to possession by a demon. With the expansion of medical science, and the increased understanding of human physiology, such a general cause for human ailments, mental and physical, has naturally been rejected by the medical profession of modern times. The disorders, however, have remained. Many of these disorders of the mind, as described in ancient and in biblical times, appear similar to those with which we are familiar today. Those states which were then said to be the result of demon-possession are now termed 'neuroses' or 'psychoses'. A man, who in the past, was thought to have been invaded by a devil, and who today would be said by a layman to be insane, is described by medical specialists as suffering from a more or less acute form of mental illness.

Modern medicine is increasingly conscious of the impossibility of making a hard and fast separation between the physical, the mental and the spiritual components of a human being. It has even been stated in the *British Medical Journal* that 'No tissue of the human body is wholly removed from the influence of the spirit' (quoted from L. D. Weatherhead, *Psychology, Religion and Healing*).

A great many instances of people, formerly understood to have been possessed by devils, have now been explained as cases of wrong functioning of the mind, sometimes owing to physical causes, sometimes to conditions of extreme mental strain, sometimes to hysteria or to autosuggestion. A diagnosis of severe mental sickness can be made where these disorders of the mind have features that are constant in all similar cases, whatever the background of the patient and whatever his social conditions, and where the development and the consequences of the disorder can be foreseen, and where a similar type of treatment and cure has been previously used.

Freud's work on the subconscious mind also created new attitudes towards mental aberrations and breakdowns. That which, in ancient days, was held to be an invasion by a spirit from without, is now seen as the result of an emotional complex, long repressed into the subconscious and at this particular moment breaking forth. The 'ego' is understood to react to this by trying to disassociate itself from the breakthrough, using different mechanisms – either what is termed 'introjection' or what is termed 'projection'. In the first, the 'ego' would identify itself with some extraneous personality, for instance some historical or mythological character; in the second, it would disown the emotional complex by assuming that there is a foreign personality dominating it. The condition of the man who was believed, through the work of a demon, to have become a totally different person, or of the man whose whole being appeared to have been taken over by a demon or by several demons, could now be explained in psychiatric terms, without the need to postulate any external supernatural force.

Innumerable cases of mental disintegration, previously thought to be the direct work of an invading demon, have been shown to be due to natural causes. But nevertheless there still seem to be, according to the churches and even to some members of the medical profession itself, rare cases, which remain inexplicable without invoking some kind of supernatural intervention. In 1948, a German physician, Doctor Alfred Lechter said in his book *Zur Frage der Bessernheit*:

> There is no doubt in my mind concerning the occurrence of actual possession, even in our own day, though such a thing is admittedly rare. I, myself, have seen a number of cases in the course of my practice which could not adequately be explained in terms of psychology or psychiatry. I waited for a long time before diagnosing possession and invariably tried to see whether some other explanation would not fit the facts, but no such explanation was to be found. (Quoted from Alois Wiesinger, *Occult Phenomena in the Light of Theology*.)

Contemporary Christian writers and preachers are fearful of anything that might seem to be irrational or superstitious in their expositions of Christian teaching. So, questions concerning devil-possession are not often discussed in sermons and theological treatises. But the questions remain, as Clifford Longley notes: '. . . it is also significant that the official churches never quite officially disown such ideas. Commissions and committes and experts, expressing the consensus of the professionally non-credulous, never quite manage, when they study this area and report back from time to time, to dismiss all of it out of hand ('The Demon that Defies Rationalism', *The Times*, 2 June 1986).

So the Christian churches, while admitting that cases of real devil-possession are extremely rare, still accept that they are possible, have existed in the past and may exist now. The idea, dating from the last century, that no psychic life exists except in connection with a material vehicle and that there can be no bodiless spirits existing in our world, had no meaning in earlier times. It is a modern conception. Traditional Christian theology has always maintained that a spirit-world exists. It has always insisted that the wording of the New Testament gives credence to the possibility of devil-possession, and indeed, makes it a fact that must be accepted, even though this may very seldom be mentioned from the pulpit today.

There is continuous reference to the 'casting out of devils' in the New Testament. The Gospels make a clear distinction between the curing of physical illnesses and disabilities, and the curing of mental and spiritual disorders which were thought to involve possession (See Matthew 4:24). It is only in the latter cases that Christ, or the Apostles, attack the cause of the disorder as an enemy, and address it as a person.

At the time of Christ, in Palestine, exorcism, or the casting out of demons, was a recognised and reputable profession. In replying to the Pharisees' accusation of using the chief of devils to cast out devils, Christ said, 'If I by Beelzebub cast out devils, by whom do your sons cast them out?' (Luke 11:19). When the disciples were sent out on their missions of preaching and healing, they were given power over devils and power to cure diseases (Luke 9:1). Following the wording of the New Testament, therefore, the Christian Churches assume belief in the power of demonic forces to invade the human psyche.

There are three cases of the 'casting out of devils' which are described in detail in the Gospel of Mark: the man in the synagogue who was heard to shriek and seen to tear and claw at himself before he was returned to normality (1:23-6); the man from 'the country of the Gaderenes' who, desperate and violent, was subject to a multitude of interior tormentors (5:1-15); and the boy who periodically fell to the ground or into the fire, foaming at the mouth (9:17-27). It has been said by writers on psychology and psychiatric medicine that the New Testament writers were using different terminology for the identical cases with which we are familiar at the present time. Today, the condition of the man in the synagogue might be diagnosed as pathological hysteria, that of the man from the country of the Gaderenes as acute manic depression, and that of the boy, almost certainly, as epilepsy. But, even when these terms are used and it thus appears that modern science can explain this type of occurrence without recourse to any demonology, there is much that is not understood about the human brain, the human mind and the human psyche. There remains, therefore, a large degree of uncertainty over what is the cause and the meaning of these strange types of disorder.

Though the nature of an epileptic sickness can now be

detected through electric apparatus, it is still not known exactly what it *is* nor how to cure it. How the nervous system of the body connects with the mind and the emotions is still unknown. Where a total change of moral personality seems to have taken place through a malfunctioning of mental and psychic functions, this connecting area still poses unanswered questions. It does not always seem possible to find the exact physiological cause for the malfunction. Whatever expression is used to describe these disorders, there is always the sense of a danger to the sufferer that must be combated: 'Whether demons are seen as metaphysical beings or as a mythological interpretation of insanity, in both cases they are experienced by the patient as an invader who has gained possession' (S. V. McCasland, *By the Finger of God*).

The Jewish exorcist in Palestine used a procedure adapted to the ideas of his time, and, however inaccurate his interpretation of the situation, where there was complete confidence in him as a healer, his exorcism very often worked. Various rituals and formalities were used in exorcisms then and are still used today, though it has been said by a modern exorcist that: 'Ritual is the outward and visible manifestation of the inward and invisible power. The words . . . are largely for the benefit of people present. But my most effective exorcisms have been carried out without a syllable being spoken. It is pure telepathy, and once you become able to do that you have tremendous strength' (The Reverend Donald Omand, Exorcist Extraordinary, in Marc Alexander, *To Anger the Devil*). The descriptions of the healing of the 'possessed' given in the Gospels may bear some relation to this. In the Gospels, Christ is said to have cured those said to be possessed, by one direct command to the evil spirit to depart from them – a very different method from that of the contemporary exorcists – and the spoken words of the command may well have been used for the purpose of instructing the onlookers. But this is only one possible aspect of the vast and difficult story.

In the cure of 'the epileptic boy', it was shown that different inner spiritual forces were needed in different cases. The Gospel writers, in their descriptions of the healing miracles, portrayed Christ as using forces from a higher plane, operating under different laws (Luke 11:20). The powers he gave to his disciples and which he instructed them to use may well have been of this same order. It is therefore impossible to be certain how we are meant to understand the cases of 'demon-possession' as they are given in the Gospels, or how we are meant to interpret the reason for their inclusion.

Up to the second half of the second century there was no distinct body of exorcists in the Church. But from that time on, there is frequent mention by Christian writers of 'devils overthrown through the name of Jesus', and the third century saw the creation of the office of Exorcist as one of the minor orders of the Church. Sacramental and ritualistic acts and ceremonies were gradually developed. In this period, there was already a recognised method for exorcists. The sign of the Cross was made on the sufferer's head, and he was sprinkled with holy water. The exorcist asked the devil his name and adjured him not to afflict the patient any more, saying 'I exorcise thee, unclean spirit, in the name of Jesus Christ; tremble, O Satan, thou enemy of the faith, thou foe of mankind' (quoted from L. D. Weatherhead, *Psychology, Religion and Healing*).

In 1614, Pope Paul V requested a publication of the *Rituale Romanum* used in the methods and ceremonies of exorcism, and the rite then formulated has remained the accepted rite until the present day.

One of the most important instructions given in the *Rituale Romanum*, and one that had already been strongly stressed, was the need to examine extremely critically all information given concerning the patient, and not to believe too early that this particular case was necessarily one of 'demon-possession'. The Synod of Rheims in 1583 had stated that an exorcist must enquire into all aspects of a patient's life, since 'sometimes the credulous and melancholic were more in need of a doctor than an exorcist'. It was also said that those who had fallen into bad ways had been known to excuse their wickedness by swearing that they were possessed by devils. Imagination of all kinds was seen to play a part, and the accepted picture of the behaviour of demons could make the patient act in an identical way.

The Manual of Exorcism of the *Rituale Romanum* gave further instruction. The exorcism must always be carried out in the name of God, and of Jesus Christ. The exorcist was warned that he was dealing with an astute adversary, strong and evil. Therefore he must have absolute confidence in God and in Jesus Christ. He must compose himself inwardly; fasting and prayer were recommended.

Then followed more external instructions. The exorcism should take place in a church or other consecrated place, and only in urgent cases should it be performed in a private house. Women and children must be excluded and also the merely curious, but there should be witnesses. It was for the exorcist to decide whether the exorcism should take place in public or not.

The ritual – and this is used today – is in five parts: prayer, an exorcism, prayer, another exorcism, and then prayer with readings from the Scriptures. The exorcism could last days, weeks and even years. The ritual actions include making the sign of the Cross, the winding of the priest's stole round the neck of the patient, the laying on of hands and the sprinkling with holy water. The exorcist must always address the spirit who has taken possession, not the patient. Above all, he must have complete trust in what he is doing and through whom he is doing it.

There is one further essential in the *Rituale Romanum*: it is stated that the office of Exorcist, which applies to all priests, only empowers performance of the rite of 'ordinary exorcism', that is to say the exorcising of the Devil in the rite of Baptism. In cases of supernatural possession, the Church uses 'Solemn Exorcism', and ordinary priests are not allowed to practise this at will. The only people authorised to exorcise the possessed are priests especially deputed to this office.

Because, as the *Rituale Romanum* was careful to emphasise, it is difficult to be certain whether or not the case to which the priest is called is truly one of demon-possession, the exorcist must know how to recognise it. There are several signs given in order to help him distinguish a state of possession from one of mental disorder.

There were originally three major signs. One was the use of a language previously totally unknown – 'the making and understanding of long speeches in tongues which are unknown to the possessed person'; another was the knowledge of hidden or distant facts or objects; and the third was the exhibition of physical powers, exceeding those natural to the age and condition of the subject. The latter two signs are of less relevance today, now that cases of clairvoyance, telepathy and telekinesis are being increasingly investigated. There are also attested instances of objects being lifted during spiritualist séances in a seemingly inexplicable manner. But the first sign is still thought to have value. Occasionally, in states of trance, strange words, possibly remaining in the subconscious and remembered from a long time past, are uttered. But there seems to be no known case of a person in a simple trance-state, hypnotic or otherwise, making ordered sentences in a language normally unknown to him, or being able to conduct a continuous conversation in that language.

One hears of cases and has read of many in the past where a man or a woman appears to those around them to have assumed another character, and usually a very unpleasant one. There are instances where young girls, normally quiet and well-spoken, suddenly speak in a harsh, masculine voice, using repulsive and obscene language. There are cases where normally religious people act with horror and hatred towards all religious objects and sacred words. To the onlookers, all these manifestations appear to be clear signs that there has been an invasion by an evil spirit. Today, there are explanations for many of these occurrences, using the language of psychiatry – repression, hysteria, schizophrenia.

In earlier times, when the existence of demons was generally accepted, the sufferer and the people around him would be certain to assume that all types of insanity and mental derangement were caused by the invasion of devils. Parts of the deranged person's personality might even act out the role which belief had created for an evil being to play, and he could very easily come to believe that he was, indeed, himself a demon. The general beliefs of these times, therefore, led to a great number of instances of 'devil-possession' being recorded; and the assumption, and therefore the trusting belief, that the exorcising priest and the holy rites which he employed had complete power over evil, resulted in innumerable cures being recorded also.

In the present day, although there are books which tell of numerous strange and inexplicable cases of evil manifestation and seemingly supernatural ways of dealing with them, the Christian Churches still maintain that authentic cases of devil-possession are extremely rare. They emphasise this strongly, because they have always held the process of exorcism to be a dangerous one, both for the exorcist and for the one to be exorcised. It is insisted that exorcism must only be used when the condition is found to be outside the bounds of recognised mental illness, because otherwise it can do the patient irreparable harm. The exorcist must, as the *Rituale Romanum* insists, be appointed for this duty, be trained for it, be trained in diagnosis, always accept medical help, and, presumably, be endowed with psychic gifts. Unfortunately, these injunctions are not always observed, and there has been a tragic incident (the Barnsley case in 1982), where unqualified people belonging to a religious cult attempted to exorcise a mentally disturbed member of their group, with disastrous results – driving him to madness and murder.

Exorcism is also said to involve strain and even danger for the exorcist himself. Whatever is 'possessing' the patient – evil spirit or evil part of the 'ego' – the exorcist has to use all his moral and psychic strength to overcome it. In the established rites of exorcism, the invader – 'demon' or 'perversion' – is directly addressed by the exorcist, so there must always be a struggle between two antagonistic spiritual entities. In the Gospels, the demons within a possessed person are described as being intensely hostile to Christ. In those times, it was believed that a name held great power. It might be that, by naming Christ as 'the Holy One of God', the demons were held to be crying out his secret name so that they might defeat his power (Mark 1:24). Those who thought themselves to be 'possessed' would have been brought up in the belief that the Messiah, when he came, would overcome all demons. Psychologists have interpreted these 'demons' as distorted sides of the personality. Thus it could be said that, in their abnormal state, with intensely heightened emotions, the sufferers felt that they recognised the promised Messiah, who would inevitably destroy the 'demons' which they imagined themselves to be. However exorcism of evil is understood, whether in past history or in the present, and whatever meaning is given to the word, it clearly involves a struggle between a force of destruction and a will to cure.

The Christian Churches, as has been shown, have always held that the most saintly people are those most attacked by demonic forces. It is, in any case, certain that the most saintly have the fiercest inner struggles, and are the most sensitive and alive to spiritual influences. Stories about attacks by demons have been attributed to saints throughout history. The most famous stories, in relatively recent times, concern the Curé d'Ars, John Vianney, who lived in the eighteenth century. It was said that people who felt themselves possessed by evil would come from miles around to be cured by him, as they felt that his goodness would drive away all wickedness; and it certainly did. The trust which he engendered and the power of his loving kindness had this effect, however the evil was understood. But he, himself, was subject to what seemed to be attacks from supernatural forces for long years of his life. His cottage was full of shouts and knocks and strange noises, his bed-clothes were ripped and his bed set on fire. These occurrences were witnessed by neighbours, who were able to swear to their objectivity. The people were certain that it was the Devil, trying to hinder the work of the good Curé. The Curé, himself, very soon accepted these troublesome manifestations as something he had to live with, and gave the presumed diabolic source of them the nickname of the 'Grappin' – 'the grappling-iron of the Devil'.

It has been thought that the 'Grappin' was some form of poltergeist. But this explains little, since it is not known what poltergeists are, although their existence has been attested by many, and their activities seem to follow a pattern. Their source of energy, by which they move objects around, is totally mysterious, as is where they come from or to where they disappear. But they are usually considered to be nondescript and neutral, neither diabolic nor angelic. According to one theory, poltergeist phenomena may be caused by unresolved tensions in the psyche of those in the neighbourhood who are unconsciously producing them. Poltergeist phenomena usually manifest when there are young adolescents in the house, an age-group liable to conflict and tension. So it is thought that deeply religious people, who are bound to suffer inner conflict, may also project their spiritual tension in this way. The Curé d'Ars had great inner conflicts to endure for many years; in the last six months of his life the inexplicable manifestations stopped.

'Demonic attacks' from without, in whatever way they are expressed, are clearly very different from what appears to be a case of 'possession' or 'invasion': 'No person who is resolved not to be possessed can be; no person consciously fighting against evil can be overcome by evil, just as a person cannot be hypnotised against his or her will' (The Reverend Donald Omand, Exorcist Extraordinary in Marc Alexander, *To Anger the Devil*). This statement was used here with particular reference to the possible danger that, when evil was driven out in an exorcism, it could enter an unsuspecting being, unaware of the nature of evil. For this reason, the Exorcist Extraordinary would not allow small children, animals or sceptics to be present at such a ceremony, because they could have 'no defence against something that they do not think exists'. The prohibitions in the *Rituale Romanum* must have had the same reasoning behind them (women then being thought to be unversed in these matters), and it is possible that the story of the Gadarene swine in the Gospels is in some way connected with this same idea.

In the Gospels, the 'possessed' people are not themselves spoken to harshly; it is only the devils within them who are rebuked. The same type of mental derangements, today, are considered to be illnesses. But it seems that interior tendencies do play a part, and there may be a type of weakness in the psyche that is liable to such dangers. Modern medicine is aware of the physical and pathological conditions that result from long and deep-seated emotions of jealousy, hate, fear, worry and resentment. All these are, in a sense, inner 'demons', or could certainly be used by any demonic force that may exist.

Another 'ally of the Devil' is imagination. It is all too easy for the mind to be a prey to superstition, and then the imagination can create havoc within. When this is connected with a hysterical condition, there are bound to be hallucinations, delusions and behaviour that has every appearance of devil-possession. In a sense, where this happens, there is no need for a diabolical power to take action. Hysteria is known to be contagious, and the famous cases in history where whole communities were said to have been taken over by the Devil, such as that of the nuns of Loudun, were most probably cases of this sort.

Satan is known primarily as 'the Tempter'. This is because the power of suggestion is perhaps the most dangerous power that humankind has to guard against. Suggestion may lie at the root of all cases of 'devil-possession', both within the deranged mind of the sufferer and within the minds of those surrounding him. Whether there is or whether there is not an external evil spirit who can possess a human being, these different types of suggestion have terrifying force. Their effects can certainly appear as the work of an unclean spirit.

# CHAPTER 13

# The Devil in Literature

Although ideas and beliefs concerning the Prince of Darkness may have been continuously changing throughout the ages, attempts to envisage and portray him have been made for centuries in all types of literature and drama. The figure of the Prince of Darkness has long held a fascination for poets and writers of the West. There have been portraits of him which have influenced the thinking of others, and there have been portraits which express ideas about him, perhaps impossible to make understandable in any other way. Among all these literary works, there are three that seem outstanding – Milton's Satan in *Paradise Lost*, the Lucifer in Dante's *Inferno*, and the Devil of *The Brothers Karamazov* by Dostoevsky.

The Satan of *Paradise Lost* is the most well-known, at least in the English-speaking world, and so has had the greatest impact on later conceptions of the Prince of Evil. Because of the grand scale of the poem and the superb beauty of its language, the impression made by Milton's Satan has had lasting effect.

The central aim of the great epic poems, *Paradise Lost* and *Paradise Regained*, was directly stated by Milton:

> That to the highth of this great Argument
> I may assert Eternal Providence,
> And justifie the wayes of God to men,

and he assuredly set out to show that misuse of the Free Will given to the angels and to humankind was the cause of all subsequent punishment and disaster. But in Milton himself there were conflicting attitudes and conflicting beliefs of which he may or may not have been aware.

The climate of opinion of the age in which Milton lived was becoming increasingly rationalist and increasingly confident in the ability of human knowledge to scale all heights. Milton was imbued with a strong belief in Scripture and in the importance of the actual wording of Scripture, but he was also a man of his age and influenced by the opinions of his age. He was rooted in a sense of Puritan righteousness and the need for discipline, but, at the same time, central to all his political ideas was his hatred of tyranny and of the oppression of free opinion. It was this double conflict which caused Milton's Satan to become a different figure from his author's theological conception of him, and to be seen by readers of the poem in a different light from that of Milton's originally avowed intention.

Though Milton portrayed Satan as rebelling for the wrong reasons, 'for Pride and worse Ambition', though Satan is essentially shown as the fiend moved by malice and revenge to bring 'Death into our world and all our woe', and though he is 'the false dissembler' and the epitome of

> *Hypocrisie, the only evil that walks*
> *Invisible, except to God alone,*

he is yet given a magnificence, equal to that of the Archangel, Michael:

> *High on a throne of Royal State, which far*
> *Out shone the wealth of Ormus and of Ind . . .*
> *Satan exalted sat, by merit raised*
> *To that bad eminence.*

Milton's fierce sense of the need to champion the right of every man to his own opinion, and his dislike of anything that savoured of despotism in government led him, perhaps even without realising it, to make God, the omnipotent and omniscient Ruler of the World, into an autocrat, ready to crush any sign of independent revolt. And so the rebellious one, who dared to defy the All-powerful, almost inevitably became a tragic hero, whose persistent refusal to submit evokes admiration for his courage and sympathy for the terrible punishment inflicted on him.

Strangely, Satan, the arch-fiend and focal point of evil, even has stirrings of conscience, as he gazes at Eden, the heavenly Paradise.

From Milton's *'Paradise Lost'*. J.B. Medina, 1688.
Warburg Institute

> *Now conscience wakes despair*
> *That slumbered, wakes the bitter memorie*
> *Of what he was, what is, and what must be*
> *Worse; of worse deeds, worse sufferings must ensue.*

He knows full well what he has done, what he has lost, what he now is.

> *. . . since against his, thy will*
> *Chose freely what it now so justly rues . . .*
> *'Which way I fly is Hell; myself am Hell.'*

He even feels remorse and pity for his followers

> *. . . condemn'd*
> *For ever now to have their lot in pain,*
> *Millions of Spirits for his fault amerc't*
> *Of Heaven.*

Thus, when he addresses them in their great assembly,

> *Thrice he assayd, and thrice in spite of scorn,*
> *Tears such as Angels weep, burst forth.*

These hints of good in what was meant to be the portrayal of wickedness incarnate are part of the false picture that Milton gave of Evil. Still more seductive are the splendid and beautiful words Satan so often uses to explain to his followers how he and they must remain faithful in their opposition to the Divine tyrant. The speech of Satan in the great debate among the leaders of the rebel armies is a clarion call to all those who feel that they are fighting the oppressors of the suffering portion of mankind.

> *'. . . What though the field be lost?*
> *All is not lost; the unconquerable Will,*
> *And study of revenge, immortal hate,*
> *And courage never to submit or yield:*
> *And what is else not to be overcome?'*

Unfortunately, 'Romantics', from the days of Byron and Shelley onwards, have been intoxicated with this picture of the Prince of Darkness. The Devil and his followers are given the glamour of those who dare and of those who fight for liberty, so that there is total confusion as to the meaning of evil. Whether the Devil is understood as the personification of what is truly evil or whether as the actual instigator of it, such a portrayal cannot be of him. The 'Romanticised Devil' has no use except as part of the beauty of a poem. The romantic poets prided themselves on their false 'devilry', and it was in this vein that Blake described Milton in *The Marriage of Heaven and Hell*: 'The reason Milton wrote in fetters when he wrote of Angels and God, and at liberty when of Devils and Hell, is because he was a true Poet and of the Devil's party without knowing it.'

The picture of Lucifer in Dante's *Inferno* is a totally different one. In a sense, he is the complete opposite to the Satan of *Paradise Lost* – no magnificence, no fierce aggression, no grand and stoical endurance. The evil of which he is the portrayal is of true horror, the negation of all creativity and life-giving power. Here the figure of the Prince of Evil certainly evokes no feeling of admiration for a daring rebel; it does not even evoke a feeling of pity for his dreadful plight, for not only is he made repulsive but also ludicrous. Having 'dared to raise his brows against his Maker', Lucifer's body, falling head-first from Heaven, plunges through the earth to its centre, where it remains immobile, head downwards, trapped in frozen ice. Dante describes him as impotent and isolated, and in complete contrast to the energy and force of God's light and love, from which he has for ever cut himself off. Each circle of the Inferno descends, becoming ever darker and narrower, until Lucifer is reached, the dead weight of sin having sunk to the centre of purposelessness.

The physical description of Lucifer was probably given by Dante to show him as a parody of God, and of the angelic host. His head has three horrible faces of three different colours, red, yellow and black – possibly as a perverted parallel with the Trinity. Each face has two wings beneath it. Lucifer, by tradition, belonged, before his fall, to the order of the Seraphim, who were said each to have six mighty wings. So Satan kept his wings, but, as in traditional images of the Devil, they had now become the bald, leathery wings of a bat.

Very different are the tears of Dante's Lucifer from those shed by the Satan of *Paradise Lost*:

> *He wept from his six eyes, and down three chins*
> *Were dripping tears all mixed with bloody slaver.*

Such ugly weeping makes Lucifer contemptible, and far from a tragic figure arousing compassion. The emotional impression given is of hopeless futility.

The loss of hope is the sole connection between the plight of Lucifer and the punishment of Milton's Satan. The regions to where Satan and his host are banished in *Paradise Lost* are

> Regions of sorrow, doleful shades, where peace
> And rest can never dwell, hope never comes
> That comes to all;

But, for Milton's Satan, even the loss of hope has an active, positive ring as if he feels that he has gained something from it, and that the evil which he now embraces has its own force and power. For by this evil he hopes to hold 'Divided Empire with Heav'ns King', and begin his work for the active ruin of mankind.

> 'So farewell Hope, and with Hope farewell Fear,
> Farewell Remorse: all Good to me is lost;
> Evil be thou my Good.'

In the Inferno, the gateway to Hell is unlike this. It shows nothing but despair. There is only what is negative; for, to Dante, in accordance with the philosophy of Neoplatonism, evil was a lack, the absence of everything positive and creative.

> 'Through me the way is to the land of pain,
> Through me the way is to eternal woe,
> Through me the way is to the ruined souls.
> By justice was my heavenly maker moved;
> I was created by the power of God,
> Supernal wisdom and primordial love.
> Before me were created only things
> Eternal, and eternal, I endure.
> All hope abandon, ye who enter here.'

Those last words have become synonymous with Hell.

Dante does not conceive Lucifer as entering our world and cunningly enticing souls into sin, but he is seen as a magnet in the centre of the earth, acting like a force of gravity, and, by the dead weight of their sins, drawing human souls into everlasting ruin.

Although, in the *Inferno*, individual, historic personalities are described in their various circles of punishment, the scale of the *Divine Comedy*, the journey of the human soul through Hell and Purgatory to Heaven, is a cosmic one. Dante describes

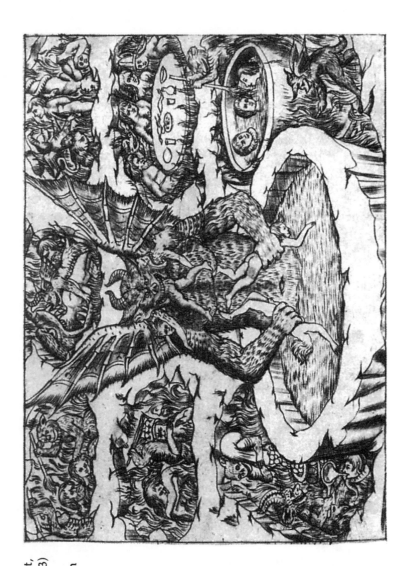

*Hell.* Florentine Print,
1477. Hind, A.V.I. (3)
pl 161.
The British Museum

the cosmos, not in purely physical terms, but as having an ethical and spiritual meaning. Above the earth are the planets and the fixed stars, and the sphere that moves the whole universe. Beyond is Heaven, the dwelling-place of God, the angels and the blessed. Dante aimed to portray the inner moral meaning of the universe, not its physical manifestations. For him, the cosmos was not neutral, but in a constant state of tension between Good and Evil. The Devil is portrayed as the focal point of evil in the universe, isolated from the force of life that moves the Sun and the Stars and that creates a living whole.

The Devil in the *Inferno* is not characterised as the Tempter and Seducer – as the being which numerous people from different eras and different countries have felt to be directly and personally attacking *them*. This last type of personification is given in the third of the great portraits – the Devil who appeared to Ivan, in *The Brothers Karamazov*.

Dostoevsky's Devil, like Dante's Lucifer, though on a totally different scale, is in direct contrast to the heroic Satan of *Paradise Lost*. He is everything that is mean and sordid. Dostoevsky deliberately makes him down-at-heel and vulgar. His check trousers are 'too tight for the present fashion' and his linen not over-clean. Everything he says is smartly clever, but trivial. The essence of this Devil lies in his power to drag all things down to the lowest possible level. He is the slanderer.

The portrayal of the Devil as low and hasty, without the slightest hint of grandeur in him, makes considerably more sense as a personification of the evil in the world than the grandiose Devil of the Romantics. But it is not only in this more intelligible conception of a spirit of evil that Dostoevsky's portrait is of value. He puts into dramatic form the endless, mysterious question – does the source of evil come from within human beings, or are they led into evil through some force independent of them?

Ivan Karamazov tries desperately to convince himself that the figure of the Devil who is talking to him and who seems to be twisting everything that he says into another meaning is part of a nightmare and has no objective existence. The Devil deliberately tries to confuse him by trotting out stories and philosophical theories that turn out to be ideas which Ivan has himself had in the past.

In his state of nightmare and tortured conscience, Ivan, at

the same time, wants to believe that there is something not himself that is forcing him to act in a way that is bound to lead to harm. He wants to believe that the responsibility is not his own. He says to his brother, Alyosha, 'I should be awfully glad to think that it was *he* and not I.' But when he talks to the figure of the Devil which he sees in his room, he puts into words the deepest feelings of those who have felt temptation towards doing what they know to be wrong: 'You are the incarnation of myself, but of one side of me . . . of my thoughts and feelings, but only the nastiest and stupidest of them, ' and again, to his brother, 'And *he* is myself, Alyosha. All that's base in me, all that's mean and contemptible.'

The portrait of Ivan's Devil shows the sordidness of evil. He becomes the embodiment of what Ivan feels to be the low and repulsive side of human nature, and also of the ambiguity that is a part of all thoughts and ideas concerning the conception of him. In the novel, he is certainly part of a nightmare dream. The glass of water which Ivan thinks to have thrown at him is on the table when he talks to Alyosha, and the wet towel, which Ivan is sure that he wrapped around his aching head, is found folded and dry in the cupboard. Nevertheless, the torment within Ivan makes it feel to him as if there is a Devilish being there attacking and arguing with him. It feels to him that if you once allow yourself to listen for a moment to the casuistic suggestions of this being, he becomes the master in the battle. So Ivan's encounter with the Devil is both a convincing portrait of the evil in the world around us, and a vivid description of the sensations of someone struggling with it. Even the sense of delirium and nightmare can often be included in the struggle.

Both Milton and Dante almost certainly accepted and did not question the existence of an independent Spirit of Evil, enemy of God and Man. Milton based much of his thinking on the literal reading of Scripture and aimed, in *Paradise Lost*, at a vast and comprehensive theodicy. Dante drew upon Christian tradition and the writings of the Scholastics for his description of Hell and of Lucifer in the *Inferno*. His powerful and terrifying picture of the focal point of Evil was related to the philosophy of the Neoplatonists and to the Scholastics. Dante's Lucifer was the Universal Evil that opposes the Divine plan for the evolution of the universe. The stories told in both these great poems were devised on a cosmic scale.

In *The Brothers Karamazov* we are on a human scale, and there is no longer a certainty of belief in an exterior, existing Devil. But 'the Devil', however he is understood, who insinuates himself into the thoughts and actions of individual human beings, is the Devil whom it is perhaps more possible for us to study, and who is almost certainly more relevant.

# CHAPTER 14

# The Psychological Devil
# and the Individual

The word 'Devil' appears in everyday speech, often almost unconsciously: 'Whatever Devil has got into him?', 'She is crying like the very Devil', 'Who the Devil do they think they are?' Even in sermons and in writings concerning spiritual temptations and struggles, the word 'Devil' is used half-consciously – in the sense that it has become a part of normal speech rather than a belief. Christian preachers and writers do not wish to include in their explanations of Christian doctrine anything that might savour of ancient superstition. As Clifford Longley writes: 'Evil is now used as an emotive word to describe extremely inhumane or antisocial behaviour, not as a thing in itself. There is no conceptual language for talking about evil detached from personal behaviour, in the way that is implied by the term "demon", or the idea of "casting out" ' ('Demon that defies Rationalism', *The Times*, 2 June 1986). But even if there is no concept of an independent force of evil, there still remains the sense, for many people, of unexplained impulses and urges to do or say those things which they know to be harmful to themselves or to others around them.

Most people probably do not feel that every time they give in to their weaknesses or indulge in antisocial behaviour they are encountering the Devil. But, at certain distinct moments in their lives, it may seem that something – whether within themselves or without, but nevertheless 'something' – is encouraging them to do or to think things of which they are ashamed. Sometimes it seems as if they are being urged to destroy, it may be by words alone, what is of the greatest value to them. Sometimes they may feel as if they are being encouraged to take no action when they witness another bringing about this kind of destruction, even to take pleasure in it – a pleasure which, it later seems to them, is entirely contrary to their normal nature. Sometimes it seems that they are drawn to enter places or to meet with people where they know they will be putting themselves under harmful and degrading influences, and yet they go. Whether these suggestions and impulses are their own, or whether they come from somewhere apart from them is the problem expressed in the agonising nightmare of Ivan Karamazov.

The word 'Devil', today is often used as an expression for the sum total of all the most unpleasant and most destructive tendencies in human beings. But whether the word is used glibly or seriously, it seems always to contain a question-mark.

On the psychological, individual human scale, the concept of the Devil as Tempter only has relevance for a human being who has a sense of right and wrong, a sense of 'good and bad' within himself and in relation to the progress of his life. It has a meaning for him if he is concerned with his better or worse relation to others and the 'good and bad' for them. If the concept of the 'Devil' is understood as 'persuasion to evil', then an aim towards a contrary 'good' must be assumed. That is to say, if a person is indifferent to any inner progress or regress in himself or to the happiness or unhappiness of his fellows, he will have no sense of 'temptation to evil'; he will not have this experience. Where there is no desire for development towards 'good', there will be no sense of obstruction in this development or of temptation towards its contrary. It seems necessary, therefore, to connect the psychological concept of the Devil with struggling humanity – with humanity that really is struggling.

In Jewish, Christian and Muslim literature, it is pride, the worship of his own ego, that caused Lucifer, the Light-bearer, to fall and become the Devil, enemy of God and Man. The myth of Lucifer's Fall was primarily used to portray the destructive force of ego-worship; the Fallen Angel then bequeathed this ego-worship to humankind. Viewed in such a light, the Devil, as the embodiment and focal point of evil, can have practical meaning only in connection with the human psyche. As Ouspensky says, 'The Devil can only manifest through the help of Man . . . Maybe when Man was invented, the Devil was invented also.'

The embodiment or, alternatively, the symbol, of evil is often mentioned in Sufism, which represents the mystical element in the Muslim religion, Islam. Here the focal point of evil is termed sometimes 'Satan' and sometimes 'Eblis'. The Sufi idea of Satan, or Eblis, is closely connected with the idea of attachment to the ego. Satan is used as a symbol for the ego and its passions, and also to describe the corrupting power that enters a human being *through* its attachment to its ego and *through* its passions:

> Every day the passions don three hundred and sixty styles of divine dress, inviting the wayfarer to go astray, but unless the passion for sinning manifests itself in one, Satan cannot penetrate the heart and inner being of the way-farer. When the predisposition for the passion arises, Satan seizes and promotes it, projecting it upon the heart; this is what is known as 'temptation' (Quoted from the Sufi writings in Dr Javad Nurbaksh, *The Great Satan 'Eblis'*).

As in so many writings on the Devil, when he is taken as the Tempter and Seducer of individual human beings, there seems, in these Sufi teachings, to be a continuous interchange of language between the description of evil tendencies in the human psyche and the description of an evil influence which can use them. The Sufis emphasised, as the Christian Church Fathers had done, that Satan cannot make an entrance into a human soul unless the way is opened for him by the weaknesses in that soul; there must be, in a sense, a 'voluntary submission'.

All teachings concerning Satan as an evil force agree that this force can only enter a human being if there is a corresponding disposition within. Gurdjieff writes, in *Views from the Real World*: 'We have many independent enemies, but the chief and most active are vanity and self-love. One teaching even calls them representatives and messengers of the Devil himself.' The fifth column within is the cause of the submission. The Sufis would say that it is impossible for Satan to dominate anyone who had dominated his own Satan, that is, his passions. Again it is never quite certain whether the Devil is a being who exploits the wickedness that is in Man or whether he *is* that wickedness. As Nurbaksh says, 'Certain Sufi masters have considered Eblis to be the carnal soul and its tendencies. They have seen the essence of Eblis as existing in human beings; Eblis enjoys no existence in his own right.'

The original meaning of the Hebrew word 'Satan' was 'adversary', and the word can be used as a common noun, simply meaning 'an attacker'. The Sufis describe the slanderous and lying thoughts which are active in our minds as being part of Satan's host: 'The Satans are the children and followers of Eblis and are present in the form of egoistic thoughts, which lead people astray. It is they who are the "sneaking whisperer".' In the same way, 'It has been said that every man has Satan as his companion living with him' (quoted in Nurbaksh).

Since a human being is not an automaton and has some freedom of choice, there must be possibilities for harm in him as well as possibilities for good. So without doubt there are evil tendencies within human beings, and, as the Sufi writings particularly state, they are centred round attachment to the false ego: 'As long as this cur of an ego is with you, Eblis will not run from you very quickly. Eblis' blandishments are based on your own dishonesty; each and every desire in you is your Eblis' (ibid.). Again the Devil is, in a sense, Man himself; and yet it can sound as if he is not.

The Devil also has the title of The Father of Lies. In Christian, Muslim and other religious teachings, the Devil is said to have brought into the world the Lie that can distort all spiritual growth. In these teachings, the fundamental lie is contained in two false beliefs: that the imaginary picture which we have created for ourselves is our true 'I'; and that our small 'ego', our changing collection of wants and fears, all activated by external happenings, is the master of our whole being, and is permanent and free. 'In himself man is not, for he is changed and altered, if he participates not in Him, Who is the same . . . and by seeing Him Who *Is* he also, according to his measure, beginneth to be' (St Augustine, *Psalmos* CXXI). The danger, according to this understanding of the human predicament, is that Man does not see himself like this, and the Father of Lies will always encourage him to set up his ego as an idol to be placated and protected at all costs. 'Evil or the evil one is the belief – or rather, the lie – that we are nothing but our ego, and this feeling of 'I' is the point where the Devil will always catch us, unless we are extremely careful and constantly watch and pray' (J. P. Ross, *A Recapitulation of the Lord's Prayer*).

The need to renounce this all-embracing self-love was also

at the centre of Sufism. The Sufis used tales of many kinds to illustrate their teachings, and this teaching in particular. One of these tales, *The Conference of Birds*, written by the Persian poet, Farid-Ud-Din Attar in the thirteenth century, includes a story within a story that has special reference to this idea:

> 'Ah, demon-spirited, conceited fool,' exclaimed the Hoopoe, 'you have become totally drowned in egotism. The Devil has entered your head. All your perfection and virtues are mere figments of your imagination. As long as you are haunted by such devilish ideas, you will remain far away from the truth. Listen to this story.'
>
> 'One day God Almighty asked Moses to learn some secret from Eblis. Moses went to Eblis and requested him to teach him a secret. "Remember this one lesson," said Eblis, "Never say 'I'; otherwise you will find yourself in the same condition as I am." ' (R. P. Masani (ed.), Abridged Edition of *The Conference of Birds*)

The converse of those who have no sense of inner struggle and so can have no personal experience of being tempted are those to whom inner struggle is the centre of their lives. The writings of some of the Christian Saints and Mystics describe these struggles. They express their spiritual experiences often in the form of a battle against attacks by the Devil or demons. Again, in the terms they use for expressing the trials endured in spiritual warfare, there is sometimes confusion between a description of harmful tendencies within and a spiritual agency producing these harmful tendencies or playing upon them.

The enemies which the Christian has to fight have been summed up as 'The World, the Flesh and the Devil'. It has been seen that in Christian Church teaching, they are regarded as three separate entities. Temptations caused by obsession with worldly objects and ambitions, and temptations caused by slavery to the desires of the body are not, in this context, synonymous with temptations caused by the Evil One. So the Devil and his weapons of attack are seen as something other than the first two enemies. Pride and self-deception, egotism and illusion are the Devil's particular weapons.

St John of the Cross, in the sixteenth century, described the Devil as the strongest and wiliest of our enemies and the most difficult to unmask. He conceived of him as a spirit, clever and shrewd.

St John naturally concentrates on the particular wiles of the Tempter that would especially endanger a man of prayer. He writes that the Devil lies in ambush, where the soul is beginning to leave the human approach to God and is entering on divine contemplation; it is through the sensitive faculties, the imagination and the sensitive memory, that the Devil can act. All deceptions enter this way.

According to St John, the main function of the Devil, in relation to one who is attempting the religious life, is to feed him with illusions that will undermine his faith, deceive him with imaginary visions and put a mask before his own true features. The Devil will attempt to deceive him by 'pious' appearances and so distract him from reality, and keep him satisfied with his present, seemingly virtuous state: 'The worst the Devil can do is to maintain the soul in the relative when it is called to the absolute' (quoted in P.L.-M de Saint Joseph, *The Devil in the Writings of St John of the Cross*). The Devil's suggestions, however harmful, are presented under the pretext of good. He always begins by counterfeiting the work of God in the soul; as St Paul says, 'Satan himself is transformed into an angel of light' (2 Corinthians 11:14). He insinuates himself into so-called religious experiences which lead only into pride and self-complacency. In this way, St John says, the Devil 'causes the ruin of a great multitude of religious pilgrims who set out on the life of perfection'.

For St John and other writers on the spiritual life, such as Lorenzo Scupoli in his *Spiritual Combat* written in 1589, it is the danger inherent in these deceptive thoughts and desires which is important, rather than the manner in which these enemies enter the mind and heart. So, although such writers may have a firm assumption and belief that an active spirit of evil is at work, aiming to prevent any growth towards perfection, the use of the word 'Devil' in describing the cause of these obstacles is not essential to their teaching. In the same way, when they portray the temptations which beset a religious person in the form of attacks by a host of demons, this is not so much an exposition of doctrine as a vivid picture of how temptation is experienced by the person tempted.

The sensation of being the victim of attack through an onslaught of harmful thoughts and fears, coming from who knows where, does not only belong to specifically religious people and to contemplative monks and nuns. Sometimes, those struggling to emerge from a depressive illness have the feeling that, from the moment they wake up, they have to ward off these spiritual attackers or else they will find themselves back in the depth of their depressive state once more. The metaphor of a host of demons, continually trying to force an invasion first from one side then from another, seems such an accurate one that it is immaterial to the person experiencing it whether this *is* a metaphor or whether it is not something more. Metaphors concerning the Devil and his host often have such power that they do their own confusing.

Another sense in which people of today may interpret 'the Devil' is in connection with the spread of ideas which they feel to be harmful and destructive. Those, who feel that mindless violence and conscienceless greed are signs of the times and are increasing, often, almost unbeknown to themselves, hark back to the old assumptions of our forefathers and consider the world to be under the influence of the Prince of Darkness. The idea of the Devil is closely related to the idea of evil influences. Writers and philosophers may explain the concept of 'the Devil' as the sum of the harmful thoughts and emotions that come from human beings and cause the influences that seem so harmful. But there still remains, for many, the feeling that some other power, if not actually responsible for the birth of these thoughts and emotions, is certainly encouraging them to grow and spread.

For the majority of people at the present time, the word 'Devil' is almost always used rather loosely as a metaphor, and almost never as the term for an independent spiritual being, except perhaps in fantasy or in joke. And yet, even the most matter-of-fact and sceptical, have occasionally a faint suspicion that it might be dangerous to treat the possibility of a demonic presence too lightly. Round the name of the Devil lingers a vestige of superstitious fear, perhaps an echo from the past. This echo is completely superstitious because unrelated to any thought-out belief, or possible 'world-view'.

Clarification of the concept of the 'Devil', knowing exactly what one means when one uses the term, is made difficult by the accretions of superstition that have gathered round it, and by the habitual use of the word 'Devil' as a symbol for all that we consider to be evil. In fact, the meaning of the concept of the Devil is continually being 'bedevilled'.

# CHAPTER 15

# Conclusion

When speaking or writing about ideas that cannot be proved by logical thinking or physical experience, it is inevitable that analogies and metaphors are used; and, in all discussions of a philosophical, metaphysical or religious nature, it is necessary to remember the part played by language in the formation of concepts and of beliefs. This is very apparent in relation to thoughts and theories about 'the Devil'. It seems that, apart from what is given in the Scriptures of world religions and their traditions, there can be no definite assertions as to the existence or non-existence of an independent, disembodied intelligence, working to produce universal harm. But, with the history of past conceptions of the Devil at our disposal, taking into account present-day knowledge, and allowing for present-day outlook, there may be possible ways for limited human minds to approach this mysterious subject, without being confused by superstition, imagination or the mirage of symbolic language.

'The greatest trick of the Devil is to persuade us that he does not exist.' This saying by the Jesuit priest, Father Ravignan, in the late nineteenth century, sums up the ambiguity surrounding the devil-concept. It warns that there could be a danger in ignoring the possibility of a cunning Satanic enemy. At the same time it exemplifies the ambiguity surrounding all thoughts and ideas about him, since the Devil would have to exist in order to seem not to exist. The Prince of Darkness deserves his title of 'Ambiguity Incarnate', and it is this ambiguity, and the perpetual confusion between forms of expression and statements of concept or fact which make a useful way of thinking so difficult to find.

The concept of the Devil is, of course, bound up with the concept of evil. So it is essential to have a clear idea of how we are using the latter term. It is conceivable that many things which *we* consider to be evil, in another context may not be so; out of certain seeming disasters can come possible good. In the study of ideas about the Devil, it seems simplest to equate goodness with that which is creative and life-giving, and evil with that which obstructs and corrupts all creative development. This kind of meaning given to good and evil can apply on all scales: on a universal scale – a creative, evolving force opposed by an unproductive force of destruction; and, on an individual scale – the aspiration towards the fulfilment of potentiality, again opposed by something that obstructs and corrupts it.

The actual existence in the universe of a force of evil, or of a focal point of evil on a cosmic scale, clearly cannot be proved or disproved by logical mind. The idea on that scale has importance only for religious philosophy or for problems of theodicy. Any ideas about the Devil that could have a practical use, in the sense of gaining more understanding of what 'evil' is and whether there are any ways to combat it, can only be on the smaller scale of individual human life. It has been seen that, throughout the study of the Devil's many aspects, the question of scale as well as of language has to be taken into account. Individual human beings may have personal experience of an evil suggestion within themselves or the sense of an evil influence endangering those around them, and this they each have to interpret in their own way. Whether there exists a force of evil on a cosmic scale beyond the scale of human life, can only be the subject of philosophical speculation, or, for some religious believers, the subject of revelation expressed in myth.

As is the case with many religious and philosophical conceptions, any conclusion concerning an evil intelligence or focal point of evil may have to be of a pragmatic nature: 'The philosophy of pragmatism goes something like this. The mind is such that it deals only with ideas. It is not possible for the mind to relate to anything other than ideas. Therefore, it is not correct to think that the mind actually can ponder reality. All that the mind can ponder is its *ideas* about reality . . . Therefore, whether or not something is true is not a matter of how closely it corresponds to the absolute truth, but of how consistent it is with our experience' (Gary Zukav, *The Dancing Wu-Li Masters: An Overview of the New Physics*). William James, who originally expounded the philosophy of pragmatism, connected it explicitly with religious beliefs. In *The Varieties of Religious Experience* he writes: 'Both instinctively and for logical reasons, I find it hard to believe that principles can exist which make no difference to facts.' In Quantum Physics, the existence of the observer alters and therefore influences that which is observed. So, in William James' view, beliefs in a transcendental world must alter the experience of facts in this one. William James held, as the proponents of the new physics were later to hold, that all that it is possible for the normal human mind to attain is the discovery of hypotheses that work. In connection with religious life, we need beliefs that can explain our experience and enable us to make progress towards our goal. Can the assumption of the Devil's existence do this?

It can be seen, through the study of history, how the unquestioning and unthinking acceptance of the idea of an existing Satanic power, ruling a cohort of minions and ever ready to attack human beings, brought fear and suspicion into people's lives, and even resulted in persecution on a large and horrifying scale. Then came the rationalism and scepticism of succeeding centuries, which brought their own danger, that of complacency. As long as humanity was considered to be inevitably pursuing an upward progressive course, 'the Devil' was ignored. People had complete confidence in mankind's increasing powers, and were blind to the possibility of the disasters that were to overtake our world.

Now, having witnessed the many horrors that have disfigured the twentieth century, and living in the knowledge that a catastrophe, resulting from human error, may well occur, which could put an end to our civilisation, if not to all life on our planet, we are returning to the outlook of the Middle Ages. It is not unusual for people to think that there may be a dangerous and evil force surrounding us, and, for some, there is a genuine fear of this evil force. But, whether an independent intelligent force exists or not, the evil that is sensed and feared can only manifest itself through individual human beings.

Since scientists are becoming increasingly aware that it is all but impossible to draw a firm dividing line between the material and the non-material, between 'matter' and 'energy', between substance and spirit, the world no longer appears to resemble a great machine, totally separate from the human psyche: 'The philosophical implication of quantum mechanics is that all of the things in our universe (including us) that appear to exist independently are actually parts of one all-encompassing organic pattern, and that no parts of that pattern are ever really separate from it or from each other.' (Gary Zukav, *The Dancing Wu-Li Masters*)

It is impossible to understand what, on a cosmic scale, a force of opposition to growth could be. But it is possible to conceive, within our planetary world, the existence of 'a something' with power to affect humanity adversely. The planetary world is understood to include the material and the immaterial. Matter, energy, human reaction, thought and perception, are all, it now seems, different ways in which the world of physics can be interpreted, depending from what aspect we view it. There is no division between spirit and matter.

Our ever-changing world is a part of a universe based on struggle, the necessary struggle of all growing things. Struggle entails something to struggle against. So among the vast complex of material and spiritual energies and forces that constitute our world, there may exist some energies that oppose our aspirations towards development. This opposing force could be seen as an extension of our own harmful thoughts and emotions, and, in that case, cannot be regarded in complete separation from them. The evil influence could thus be ourselves, but *not* ourselves. This might explain another saying about the Devil, which further elaborates Father Ravignan's warning: 'Nothing can be more dangerous than to deny the Devil's existence, which is as real – although no more so – as our own; we dare not deny Satan, until we have denied ourselves, as everyone must who would follow Him, who said and did nothing "of Himself"' (Ananda Coomeraswamy, *Selected Papers*).

Human beings tend to forget that everything that they do, say and think has some consequence for which they are responsible. On the level of human egoism and of the thoughts and emotions that are part of it, it may unfortunately be possible, through the energy of these thoughts and emotions, to co-operate with an evil energy acting in the world, and to increase and add to its power. It could have been a force such as this that has long been described as 'the Devil'.

If such an influence exists, it seems that it is the activity of suggestion which gives it its power. With all modern technology at its disposal, suggestion can never have been more powerful than it is today. This pressure of suggestion might be an indication of how the products of individual human minds could be exaggerated and possibly manipulated by an external energy. False suggestion, the Lie, has been associated with the Devil from the first appearance of that concept. This weapon of suggestion, both in the past and in the present, appears to have caused, above all, the spread of hatred – mindless hatred, vindictive hatred, hatred based on greed and envy, and, especially 'diabolical', self-righteous hatred under the guise of fighting or working for 'the good'.

Today we do not seem to be suffering to the same extent as our forebears from the danger of complacency. So that, however strong our fear of destruction and our sense of disintegration, ours is, in this particular, a hopeful age. It might even be that, because of these fears, our eyes are beginning to be a little more open, and, despite the pressure of suggestion, it is possible that we will become more alert to the evil influence that ugly emotions can produce and have produced.

If we term something 'evil', we must mean that it is totally and intrinsically undesirable, and therefore must, to the best of human ability, be combated. The original purpose, among religious leaders, for using the term, 'Devil', to epitomise and give a focus to all that was felt to be inimical to Man was to ensure that human beings would engage in a spiritual combat against this enemy, 'the Adversary'. They wanted to show that there is an enmity towards Man that is part of existence and cannot be wished away. And yet, under his names of 'Satan' and 'Eblis', legend shows 'the Adversary' actually serving ultimate good, however contrary to his own will. The struggle against him brought understanding to Job and to Moses.

We have to accept that there are wrongs within and without us that should be put right. If we think that there is an evil influence that produces or encourages these wrongs, and then consciously or half-consciously equate that influence with 'the Devil', it is essential that we should be on the alert not to be deceived by 'him'. Religious teachings about the Devil have continually warned of the necessity to be on guard against the Evil One, but insist that he cannot force anyone to sin against his will. Persuasion is his only means.

This 'Devil' can work his persuasion only through the mind and heart of an individual person. The belief that some power, extraneous to ourselves, is responsible for all our ills seems, from ancient days, to have been an illusion spread by the Father of Lies. Whether this power be called 'Society', 'Heredity' or 'The Devil and his hordes', or any other name, the illusion is the same. But suggestion does not mean inevitable submission, and response to suggestion can only come through each individual, whether alone or in a body.

The force of persuasion that encourages evil may be understood as coming from within human beings or as coming from without, as the personification of the harmful tendencies that exist within human nature or as the work of an independent, hostile intelligence. All that is certain is that lies and false suggestion have the power to destroy us, if we let them, and so it is they, from wherever they come, that constitute the Dark Enemy of our world – the enemy who, from time immemorial, has been called the Prince of Darkness.

# Bibliography

Adams, Henry *Mont St Michel and Chartres* (Constable, New Edition, London, 1950)

Alexander, Marc *To Anger the Devil, The Rev. Donald Omand Exorcist Extraordinary* (Neville Spearman, Jersey, 1978)

Bennett, H. S. *Life on the English Manor* (Alan Sutton, Gloucester, 1987)

Blackettt-Ord, M. *Hell-Fire Duke* (The Kensal Press, Berks, 1982)

Bruno de Jesus-Marie O. C. D (editor) *Satan Etudes Carmelitaines* (Sheed & Ward, London, 1951)

de Bruyn, Lucy *Woman and the Devil in Sixteenth Century Literature* (Compton Press, Tisbury, 1979)

Carus, Paul *The History of the Devil and the Idea of Evil* (Bell Publishing Co, New York, 1900)

Charles, R. H. (editor) *The Book of Enoch* (S.P.C.K, 1966)

Cohn, Norman *Europe's Inner Demons* (Chatto Heinemann – for Sussex University Press, 1975)

Coomeraswamy, A. *Selected Papers* (Princeton University Press, 1977)

Evans, G. R. *Augustine on Evil* (Cambridge University Press, 1982)

Gurdjieff, G. I. *All and Everything, Beelzebub's Tales to his Grandson* (Harcourt, Brace, New York, 1950)

Gurdjieff, G. I. *Views from the Real World* (Arkana Paperbacks, 1984)

Hill, Christopher *Milton and the English Revolution* (Faber & Faber, London, 1977)

James, William *The Varieties of Religious Experience* (Longmans, Green New Impression, London, 1937)

Journet, Charles *The Meaning of Evil* (Geoffrey Chapman, London, 1963)

Ladurie, E. le R. *Montaillou* (Penguin Books, 1980)

Lamborn Wilson, P. *Angels* (Thames and Hudson, London, 1980)

Langton, Edward *Satan, a Portrait* (Skeffington and Son, London, 1945)

McCausland, S. V. *By the Finger of God (Exorcism)* (MacMillan and Co, New York, 1951)

Manschreck, C. L. *A Study of Christianity, From Persecution to Uncertainty* (Prentice Hall, Inc, New Jersey, 1974)

Mother Maria (Lydia Gysi) *Evil in the New Testament* (Greek Orthodox Monastery of the Assumption, 1973)

Musa, Mark *Introduction, Notes and Commentary on Dante's Divine Comedy* (Indiana University Press, 1971)

Masani, R. P. (editor) *The Conference of Birds* (Abridged Edition) (Oxford University Press, 1924)

Nurbaksh, Javad *The Great Satan 'Eblis'* (Khaniquahi-Nimatullahi Publications, London, 1986)

Oesterreich, T. K. *Possession, Demoniacal and other* (Citadel Press, 1974)

O'Grady, Joan *Heresy* (Element Books, Shaftesbury, 1985)

Ouspensky, P. D. *A New Model of the Universe* (Kegan Paul, London, 1938)

Ouspensky, P. D. *Talks with a Devil* (Turnstone Press, London, 1972)

Ouspensky, P. D. *A Further Record. Extracts from Meetings* (Arkana Paperbacks, London, 1956)

Rankin, O. S. *Israel's Wisdom Literature* (T. and T. Clark, Edinburgh, 1936)

Ross, J. P. *A Recapitulatin of the Lord's Prayer* (J. P. Ross, Alresford, 1985)

Rudwin, Maximilian *The Devil in Legend and Literature* (La Salle, Chicago, 1931)

Russell, J. B. *The Devil. Perception of Evil from Antiquity to Primitive Christianity* (Cornell University Press, Ithaca and London 1977)

Russell J. B. *Satan. The Early Christian Tradition* (Cornell University Press, Ithaca and London 1981)

Russell J. B. *Lucifer, the Devil in the Middle Ages* (Cornell University Press, Ithaca and London 1984)

Sheppard, L. C. *Portrait of a Parish Priest. The Curé d'Ars* (The Catholic Book Club, London, 1958)

Thomas, Keith *Religion and the Decline of Magic* (Weidenfield and Nicholson, London, 1971)

Tuchman, Barbara *The Fourteenth Century, a Distant Mirror* (Macmillan, London, 1979)

Warner, Marina *Alone of all her Sex* (Alfred Knopf, New York, 1976)

Weatherhead, L. D. *Psychology, Religion and Healing* (Hodder and Stoughton, London, 1976)

Wolf Philippe *The Awakening of Europe* (Penguin Books, 1968)

Wresinger, Alois *Occult Phenomena in the Light of Theology* (Burns Oates, London, 1967)

Zukav, Gary *The Dancing Wu-Li Masters, An Overview of the New Physics* (Fontana Press, 1984)

# Index